Praise for *The Millennial Myth*

"Crystal captures the fundamental disconnect between what people think of Millennials, misguided generalizations based on tired stereotypes that have followed every generation, and who they actually are—which is the future leaders of our workforce. At Bullhorn we've adopted a 'Millennial mindset' of our own, remaining agile, innovative, and transparent in how we operate and build software, and the impact on productivity and employee happiness has been unprecedented."
—**Art Papas, CEO, Bullhorn**

"The behaviors that result from our perceptions are real—even if our perceptions are incorrect. Crystal is clear in her eye-opening and clarifying concepts that lead to mutual understanding. The new generation entering the workforce at an accelerated pace are messengers from the future. Their presence shines a light on the way the world is becoming. To mislabel or ignore them would be detrimental to all the generations in the workforce. Crystal shows how Millennial behavior is modern behavior and will be a guide for many generations to come. You will love this book!"
—**Mick Ukleja, PhD, President, LeadershipTraQ, professor, and coauthor of**
   Managing the Millennials

"Crystal Kadakia is the champion for Millennial engagement and so much more. She spells out a compelling and thoughtful framework that goes beyond generations. Without incorporating a growth mindset, an eye for high potentials, and an ability to adapt with technological advances—which are all skills we can learn from Millennials—our businesses will become obsolete. This is bigger than generations clashing in the workplace—it's the future of business!"
—**Zulna Heriscar, Worldwide Field Partner Sales Lead, Cloud + Enterprise Division,**
   Microsoft Corporation

"When popular philosophy falls behind technological and economic advances, social institutions are at risk of failing to provide opportunity for their members—it is called structural lag. Crystal masterfully describes the effect of structural lag on Millennials and how organizations can create opportunity for an emerging workforce to have a positive influence."
—**Chip Espinoza, PhD, coauthor of** *Managing the Millennials*, *Millennials@Work*,
   and *Millennials Who Manage*

"As cofounders of Culture of Good, Inc., which inspires more than three thousand Millennial employees to do meaningful work, we found *The Millennial Myth* to be spot on. Not only has Crystal helped dispel myths that simply hold little truth about the next generation of leaders, but she has also provided in extensive detail the way forward for those leading them. This book is a must-read for those who expect to have success in leading the next generation of employees."
—**Scott Moorehead and Ryan McCarty, cofounders of Culture of Good, Inc., and**
   coauthors of *Build a Culture of Good*

The Millennial MYTH

The
Millennial
MYTH

Transforming Misunderstanding
into Workplace Breakthroughs

Crystal Kadakia

BK·

Berrett–Koehler Publishers, Inc.
a BK Business book

Berrett-Koehler Publishers, Inc.

1333 Broadway, Suite 1000

Oakland, CA 94612-1921

Tel: (510) 817-2277 Fax: (510) 817-2278 www.bkconnection.com

Ordering Information

Quantity sales. Special discounts are available on quantity purchases by corporations, associations, and others. For details, contact the "Special Sales Department" at the Berrett-Koehler address above.

Individual sales. Berrett-Koehler publications are available through most bookstores. They can also be ordered directly from Berrett-Koehler: Tel: (800) 929-2929; Fax: (802) 864-7626; www.bkconnection.com

Orders for college textbook/course adoption use. Please contact Berrett-Koehler: Tel: (800) 929-2929; Fax: (802) 864-7626.

Orders by U.S. trade bookstores and wholesalers. Please contact Ingram Publisher Services, Tel: (800) 509-4887; Fax: (800) 838-1149; E-mail: customer.service @ingrampublisherservices.com; or visit www.ingrampublisherservices.com/Ordering for details about electronic ordering.

Berrett-Koehler and the BK logo are registered trademarks of Berrett-Koehler Publishers, Inc.

Printed in the United States of America

Berrett-Koehler books are printed on long-lasting acid-free paper. When it is available, we choose paper that has been manufactured by environmentally responsible processes. These may include using trees grown in sustainable forests, incorporating recycled paper, minimizing chlorine in bleaching, or recycling the energy produced at the paper mill.

Library of Congress Cataloging-in-Publication Data

Names: Kadakia, Crystal, author.
Title: The millennial myth : transforming misunderstanding into workplace breakthroughs / by Crystal Kadakia.
Description: First Edition. | Oakland, Calif. : Berrett-Koehler Publishers, [2017]
Identifiers: LCCN 2017000739 | ISBN 9781626569560 (pbk.)
Subjects: LCSH: Personnel management. | Young adults--Employment. | Generation Y.
Classification: LCC HF5549 .K223 2017 | DDC 658.30084/2--dc22
LC record available at https://lccn.loc.gov/2017000739

22 21 20 19 18 17   10 9 8 7 6 5 4 3 2 1

Interior design and production: Dovetail Publishing Services
Cover designer: The BookDesigners

To the many who have inspired me along the way by embracing the changes in life as though they were a true friend, one who challenges you and helps you rise to greater heights.

Contents

Millennials and the Modern Workplace

I'm a female. I'm an American-born Asian. I'm a chemical engineer by training. I got my first job when I was 13 and graduated with my bachelor's when I was 20. I spent seven years working for a Fortune 50 company, beginning as an engineer and then as a training manager. I left to launch my own firm, Invati Consulting. I've given over 100 talks that have reached over 5,000 people, including two TEDx talks, on a unique intersection: millennial behavior and modern workplace culture. I've discussed challenges like modernizing to a digital workplace and generational transition with countless executives. I've developed proprietary consulting and training solutions to enable the shift to organizational designs that support modern workplace culture. I've been recognized for these achievements, including receiving the Power 30 Under 30, Association for Talent Development's One to Watch, and Chief Learning Officer's Learning in Practice awards.

Before I get hurt patting myself too hard on the back, let me share that I'm also . . . dare I say it? A millennial.

Today, I cringe at owning this part of my identity. It feels like the moment I type the word "millennial," I have somehow discounted all my other qualities and accomplishments and made them less true. Yet indeed, I am a part of this "lazy, entitled, job-hopping" generation. The most common retort to my admission is, "Oh, but you're Asian, so it's different for you." Being Asian automatically brings up preconceived notions of Tiger Moms and driven children. However, my achievements cannot solely be attributed to my Asian upbringing. My achievements are attributed to my whole self, the varied fabric that makes up me.

To explain the seemingly "un-millennial-like" behavior of the many millennials they know, older generations often find similar excuses. I've often overheard an older generation individual saying to a millennial, "You're the exception" or "I'm not talking about you, of course." These justifications seek to hide one of the largest inconvenient truths: *that perhaps the majority of millennials are not, in reality, the lazy, entitled, disrespectful, feedback-driven job-hoppers that they are often believed to be.*

When I started my career, I was just Crystal Kadakia. I pursued things like actively challenging myself, trying to make a difference in the world, and focusing on what I could do instead of what I couldn't. I wanted to bring all of that potential to work and make use of it. I didn't know back then how "millennial" I really was by single-mindedly pursuing the idea of using my potential to its highest level, including wild experiments with lifestyle and career choices with little regard for traditional structure. Today, I know that older generations perceive such behavior as millennial. But what I also know is that *this is not just millennial, but modern. I know that millennial behavior signals the behavior of generations to come.*

My passion became clear as several pieces began to collide. While in my role as a training manager at the Fortune 50 company, I had a baby boomer directly reporting to me as we designed training for new hires. Around 2010, negative perspectives on millennials were everywhere in the media. It wasn't the negativity that bothered me; it was the misalignment with reality. My boomer colleague and I would often discuss misleading media accounts about millennials, and we decided to prove them wrong in our training work. We launched several successful cross-generational programs based on what we were actually seeing, and none of them conformed to stereotypes—but these local successes didn't satisfy my drive to change the dominant stereotypes about my generation.

The proverbial straw that broke the camel's back was when I saw HR leaders, trainers, and seminar speakers espousing incorrect generational traits based on these media resources. Remember those tables of generational differences with values like hardworking or loyal for each generation, as though entire generations had a single personality? Everyone, regardless of generation, would look rather confused at the end of these training programs on embracing generational diversity. Participants often commented, "I feel like an old soul" or "I feel like a millennial at heart" were common phrases spoken by participants. People didn't fit into the neat, confining boxes being presented or learn actionable skills; the training simply reinforced attitudes based on stereotypes.

I wanted to draw new connections for people of all generations, and particularly for corporations trying to adapt to a digitally driven world. I eventually built the momentum to start Invati Consulting, where today I speak, train, and consult on this unique challenge: changing the focus of the conversation from generations and millennials to understanding modern talent behavior and the corresponding new workplace design. I discovered the audience was hungry for meaningful, actionable perspectives in this arena. Through my extensive research and my own experience as a millennial, I have established a completely different language for interpreting the behavior of my generation, recast in a new light based on the impact of digital technology. Because all society is digitally enabled today, this new understanding then provides clues for much-needed organizational changes to better engage all modern talent.

To put it another way, despite the extremely heavy focus on millennials, it's not about them. It's about what makes modern talent, in the context of today's digitally enabled environment, engaged and productive. Millennials are the first generation of "digital natives," having coming of age with computers, the Internet, and digital technology. As such, they just happen to be the best informants to strategically guide modern workplace trends, both in terms of what we should change (based on the positive behavior of millennials) and what we should bring forward from the past (based on the risks of millennial behavior). To do so, we require a high degree of objectivity and cross-generational understanding.

Unfortunately, it is this very objectivity and understanding that is missing. Over the last five years, I have extensively researched the perceptions of millennials in the workplace, why they exist, and what we should act on instead. Ultimately, the perceptions we hold today are rooted in a sensationalized media profile of an entire population. As a result, people, including senior leaders, have a tendency to transform interactions with millennials into negative experiences. For example, when asked for training and career growth opportunities, managers and leaders may automatically think, "Oh, you must be entitled. What have you done to deserve that?" This is an example of cognitive bias called confirmation bias, defined as "having a tendency to listen only to information that confirms our preconceptions."[1] Yet the millennial perspective is, "I'm entitled? Because I want to learn about how to do my job and to do it so I succeed?" Unfortunately, these misconceptions have deeply infiltrated the workplace, especially at the managerial level and higher, where the shaping of the workplace happens.

I wrote this book to spark a new discussion among leaders and managers. Instead of complaining about adapting for millennials, it's imperative for leaders and managers to acknowledge the role of millennial behavior as an indication of the needs of the modern workplace to attract, leverage, and retain modern talent. Many look at millennials as a topic related to diversity and inclusion or generational traits. Separately, others look at the topic of the future workplace. The new discussion I am launching drives an unbreakable, crucial connection between five of the most misunderstood millennial behaviors and the digitally enabled workplace revolution.

My objective is not to defend the millennial generation or present a view of what is right or wrong, good or bad, best or worst. Nor is it to focus on changing the workplace for millennials specifically. Rather, it is to provide an accurate, inclusive picture of how the world has changed and how that has impacted talent across all generations today and will continue to impact talent tomorrow.

It's about reducing turnover and increasing engagement, but also about ensuring profitability, driving innovation, and existing as a company in the future. If an organization can't engage their youngest employee base to contribute to building their vision, how can they attract their youngest customers to purchase their products? One of the biggest fears of CEOs today is to be "Uber-ized"—that is, to lose business due to a complete revolution in the way things have always been done, just as Uber has done with the public transportation industry. To overcome this fear and remain successful, more than ever before, it is vital to deeply understand and embrace the future generation. Unlocking and harnessing the potential of modern talent is the ultimate key to survival in today's global, hyper-connected, digital society.

The
Millennial
MYTH

The Perceptions We Hold Today

Every cloud has . . .
a silver lining.
The greatest invention since . . .
sliced bread.
Computing power . . .
doubles every two years.
Millennials are . . .
lazy and entitled.

Why? Why do we automatically complete this sentence with "lazy and entitled"? Why do search engines such as Google and Bing highlight these stereotypes in their autocomplete feature? Why are there a million-plus search results for "lazy and entitled" that are linked to the millennial generation? What autocomplete words do we have for other generations? And, as organizations, leaders, and coworkers, what expectations, behaviors, and contributions are we missing out on because of these biases?

Millennials, as defined in this book, are those born between 1981 and 1996. Generation Z is the generation following millennials, born in 1996 to the present, and are just beginning to graduate from college. In the last 50 years, rapid technological changes have created a vast difference between the perspectives, values, beliefs, and expectations of the older and youngest generations around the globe. The difference is so vast that we fundamentally struggle to understand the world we each come from. It's not an exaggeration to say that different generations may see the same behaviors or dynamics in the workplace and perceive completely different things, whether positive or negative. My purpose in this book is to help bridge this gap for five of the most misunderstood behaviors, especially for the senior workers and leaders for whom millennial employees and their perceived expectations so often seem mysterious.

Where Did the Perceptions Come From?

Many books, written in the past decade mostly by baby boomers and gen Xers, looked into the crystal ball and made predictions about millennial characteristics as they were growing up. Before the explosive rise of the smartphone and social media, in their seminal book published in 2000, *Millennials Rising: The Next Great Generation*, Neil Howe and William Strauss cautioned, "Nearly all of today's teen negatives are residues of trends launched by the boomers, apexed by gen Xers. Conversely, nearly all of today's teens' positives are new trends, unique to millennials, with much of the initiative coming from them."[1] Today, we continually witness the impact of negative perceptions as leaders struggle to choose between inaction and action, afraid of "pandering" to millennial expectations, rather than viewing these new perspectives as an opportunity to modernize for the common good.

Initially, the theories about millennials were presented by qualified researchers who had invested hours collecting data and distilling stories into meaningful representations. Howe and Strauss were among the first generational analysts to gain popularity. They put forth an immensely positive view of the millennial generation. Later, other generational analysts such as Jean Twenge (author of *Generation Me*) and Mark Bauerlein (author of *The Dumbest Generation*) criticized their approach and instead popularized the negative aspects of millennials. The words "narcissistic," "entitled," and "lazy" began to emerge. However, these phrases weren't just passed into society through books and articles. They were passed through social media, an exponentially viral medium, in which unreliable data and sensational messages spread like wildfire.

Millennials responded with fierce blogs, "rants," videos, and memes. Two different worlds collided: the world of the distinguished expert and the world of the digital influencer. As social media's two-way information flow grew at an enormous rate post-2000, the distinctly negative perception won out, because frankly, that is what made headlines. More than 20 articles per day are published online on the topic of millennials, everything from how they choose to vote to home-buying habits to the latest top 10 list on what is liked or disliked about them. Living in this information-bloated world, it's no wonder society at large began to parrot the drama we heard. In contrast, while every generation has dealt with complaints, gen X and boomers didn't have such a variety of high-volume, fast-paced sources of vocal discontent to contend with when they were coming of age.

Regardless, neither of these approaches, positive or negative, is fully accurate. And often, whether the writers are experts or bloggers, they simply select the formative events that best serve the idea they want to present: either that millennials will be saviors of mankind or that millennials are no more than device-controlled vegetables who expect everything to be done for them. Through the virality of social media, these crystal ball predictions have become the accepted truth, instead of being validated and confirmed. Older generations invented a tool they didn't know the full capability of: the Internet. They failed to realize the avalanche of biased blind spots and generation gaps that would be caused by their quick judgment. The root cause behind the challenges of attracting and retaining millennials in the workplace lies within this widespread avalanche of misunderstanding. What we have today is just a slice of the overall picture, presented by white papers, top 10 lists, blogs, videos, books, TV interviews, and misguided speakers and trainers.

The degree of the disservice we have done to the millennial generation through the unintended impact of social media is evident. Pew Research conducted a study in 2015 on how generations perceive themselves.[2] It's telling that only 8 percent of millennials feel the generational label describes their generation very well. Furthermore, when the study goes on to explore the traits attributed to each generation, millennials are the harshest critics of their own generation, unlike any of the other generations. Surprisingly, this indicates that millennials themselves have internalized the media's negative definition of them, but *92 percent of millennials don't identify with the labels!* There is a significant disconnect between the characteristics assumed of the millennial generation and the reality experienced by actual millennials. Evidently, the generational labels we have for millennials today are . . . mislabeled.

Like much propaganda, it's those at the top who have the most power to shape our views—and the people at the top today are boomers, equal in size to the millennial population. Ironically, generation X voiced many of the same workplace desires as millennials, but as a smaller generation, they were relegated to fighting like David against Goliath. Today, it's more equally matched and like a game of Chicken, the question is who will dodge first? Will the deeply ingrained command and control preference of traditional mindsets win out, or will the collaborative tendencies of millennials influence us to work together to shape the future of work instead?

The Business Case for Understanding Millennials

Why do we need to reset our perceptions of millennials? Every generation has to overcome negativity from the older generations, right? The new kids on the block should be the ones to adapt.

Every generation that has gone before us has thought that. And yet, every new generation has created progress through their resistance of the status quo. Eventually, the new generation's expectations, small or large, were integrated into how we work and live.

Today, integrating new expectations may seem insurmountable because they are being driven by a significant, fast-paced change in the world. Consider the significance of the time we are living in: *the millennial generation is the last generation to remember a world without the Internet.* Millennials are both the first generation to form their world perspective from a digitally influenced vantage point and the last to remember

4

what it was like not to always be connected. The Internet is such a big change to the world, the way we do things, the way we behave, that to dismiss its impact on millennials by categorizing their behavior as fleeting generational traits is a serious error in judgment. Overall, the impact to businesses that don't seek to understand millennial employees is that *they inherently will not understand how to engage generations beyond millennials*, as well as digitally enabled talent today regardless of generation.

To complicate things further, other generations had decades to get used to big changes. Consider major inventions like paper, electricity, television, and new forms of transportation like ships and trains. As these inventions became the new normal, skills, attitudes, and behaviors became obsolete, were transformed, and were created. For example, many said that the light bulb would never happen. Once it did, it transformed society by bringing about the need for larger power grids and distribution networks. Behaviorally, attitudes and expectations formed around always having light. The scope of activities we could do in the evening changed. Some activities, skills, and values were lost. However, in the past, these game changers occurred further apart and fewer between, and we had generations to get used to them. Starting with the boomer generation, changes began to come faster and faster, often within the span of a decade or two, leading to a need to integrate expectations faster.

Unfortunately, the slow integration of millennials' new expectations, driven by the combination of the innate desire to maintain status quo and the avalanche of negative, viral social media, has led to highly visible consequences. Many have become focused on either doing nothing ("We don't need to change; if it ain't broke, don't fix it") or rigidly trying to make millennials fit in with the existing paradigm ("They should adapt to us"). As a result, many organizations are already experiencing the following immediate business impacts:

> **Costs due to turnover.** Today's organizations are facing unprecedented challenges to attract and retain young talent. A 2016 study by Gallup estimated that millennial turnover costs the US economy $30.5 billion every year.[3] According to Millennial Branding's

study on millennial retention, 56 percent of millennials expect to leave their jobs in three years or less.[4] It's easy to conclude that this loss is tied to lack of understanding of modern talent needs.

> **Lack of bench strength.** Along with the costs of higher turnover, profit is at risk due to lack of a leadership pipeline. Whether hiring from external sources or developing leaders from within, lack of talent longevity creates significant skill gaps as well as a smaller talent pool of high-potential employees. Future profit requires future leaders. Future leaders want an effective, modern culture in the present, including clear personal reasons to stay at a job other than the benefit of an employer's brand name.

> **Loss of core knowledge.** There is limited time to understand what should intentionally be brought forward from previous generations. Without transferring knowledge, profit loss can be significant and unpredictable. For example, an aerospace company went through a period of early retirements to cut back on costs during the recession. A few years later, they had to shut down a plant for two weeks because of a problem no one knew how to solve. They had to hire back retirees for the fix. Although boomers will not retire en masse, transferring core competencies built over a 40-year career takes significant time. Without creating an effective cross-generational culture, critical lessons, experience, and core values will be lost that could greatly impact profit.

> **Decreased employee engagement.** Gallup's 2016 report also indicated that 55 percent of millennials are not engaged at work, the highest number of any generation.[5] Ongoing industry-wide research has proven that organizations with highly engaged employees consistently outperform organizations with disengaged employees in the marketplace. Understanding how to engage millennials and digitally enabled talent is imperative to build a high-performing organization.

› **Decreased access to top talent.** Today, many organizations are engaged in talent wars, spending millions on recruiting top talent. Organizations usually compete with each other for talent, but organizations are also at war with talent itself. For a multitude of reasons, many millennials and especially gen Z are attracted to entrepreneurship and start-ups instead of the traditional 9 to 5. According to Millennial Branding's 2014 study on high school careers, 72 percent of high school students, nearly three-quarters, want to be business owners someday.[6] Internal workplace culture can be changed to match employees' shifting expectations and thereby attract top talent.

With the many innovations in the last few decades, we have created a complex social paradigm. Older generations want younger generations to behave in a way that is congruent with how the world was—to be able to replicate today the practices that engaged and retained employees "well enough" yesterday. With the exception of a relative few, that's by and large what the generations that preceded them did: focused on assimilating the new to the old. Yet so much has changed that the gap is wide between what an older generation expects and what a younger generation knows to do or believes is right.

Moreover, the creator of the gap, digital technology, is not going away. Unsurprisingly, since we all live in this digitally enabled world, it is often said, "Millennials want what everyone wants!" If that is the case, why resist giving everyone the changes they want? Traditional-minded leaders continue complaining about the latest generation instead of engaging in the timeless generational practice of shifting from complaints to serving as mentors, showing millennials the ropes, and acknowledging forward-thinking practices. The negative perception of millennials by older generations can be validated and reinforced by the Internet and other media, stopping the inclination to offer acceptance that someone once did for older generations in their early career days. However, we can successfully navigate these uncertain, unknown waters and build a bridge into the future by fairly and thoughtfully considering both established experiences *and* new perspectives of the way we work.

Through my research, it has become clear that the changing behavior highlighted by millennials is indicative of evolving needs for all of us, that is, all digitally enabled talent. Through offering an incomplete, biased picture of millennials, we have created a critical barrier to the modernization of the workplace. The potential upside for letting go of our stereotypes, reestablishing understanding, and acting purposefully is immense. Boomers, gen Xers, and millennials can form relationships where knowledge is transferred, productivity increases, and supportive community is built. We can be better prepared to attract, engage, and retain generation Z as they enter the workplace and avoid the challenges experienced with millennials. We can feel more empowered ourselves, knowing that we are not just doing what we have always done, but are doing the right things.

Who This Book Is For: Leaders, Managers, and Change Champions

As you read on, I hope you find that this is more than just another book about millennials. Rather, it is intended to help you:

> Gain insight to make meaningful, strategic investments around modern workplace culture

> Lead efforts to build a modern, high-performing workplace

> Understand millennials better from a millennial's perspective

> Drive the connection of millennial behavior to modern workplace culture, beyond discussions of diversity and inclusion of generations

> Create a win-win, effective cross-generational culture that will enable your organization to not just survive, but thrive in the twenty-first century

This book is targeted toward global leaders at all levels, from C-suite level all the way down to frontline managers. Although written from a US vantage point, especially concerning statistics and data, the underlying millennial behaviors, themes, and concepts are intended to be as globally relevant as possible. If you are responsible for cascading culture and building the organization, this book will prove to be an invaluable resource to translating modern talent expectations into organizational culture strategies.

One of the biggest mistakes organizations make is assuming that what works for the Googles of the world will also work for them. We would like to believe that we can simply copy and paste superficial changes that appear "sexy" and that these will solve our deep engagement and productivity issues. In reality, changing the color of the walls, having snack machines, installing ping-pong tables, and moving to open office layouts, among other façade changes, are only Band-Aid solutions that do nothing to address an inevitable revolution. This book will help change champions like you understand the variety of factors related to engaging, productive modern workplaces that we can learn from millennial behavior. Armed with this new understanding, you'll be in a better position to use your deep experience wisely, while making strategic investments that are more impactful and cost-effective than putting your staff on matching bicycles.

In the last decade, the majority of books published on millennials focused on dissecting their attitudes and beliefs from a diversity and inclusion or managerial perspective. Books have also been written about the future workplace but either exclude or minimize the impact of millennial behavior. Oftentimes, this is because the authors aren't millennials and lack the understanding needed to drive the connection. Instead of leveraging millennials to understand the needs of a digitally enabled workforce, we have moved on as though generational differences were a passing fad. Senior leaders and managers find themselves in need of something practical to guide their actions, yet the search is akin to finding an oasis in the desert. We come across many mirages and are unsure of ever finding a true paradise. This book is a sharp deviation from previous works in that it seeks to start a new discussion for leaders and managers by reexamining our presumptions for five of the biggest millennial stereotypes, learning a new language, being inspired by the rewards, and enabling strategic, purposeful action.

Who This Book Is About

This book is inspired by the behavior of high-performing millennials, but it applies to modern talent as a whole. To explain what I mean by high-performing or "top talent" millennials, consider that with the advent of digital technology, some millennials (and people in general) are more capable at filtering through the overwhelming amounts of information and leveraging it to take action. Some, however, are instead overwhelmed and let technology drive them. For example, some are sensitive to digital distractions and procrastinate, lack focused attention, and exhibit other problems. While neuroscience research is ongoing to discover the cause for these differences, this book is based on the behavior of those millennials who clearly have adapted successfully. Those who have persevered through college or entrepreneurial gap years post–high school and have made it through the high hurdles of today's world-class recruiting processes are more likely to have adapted well to technology.

These top talent millennials give us clues for what works well in this digitally enabled society. They have experimented and tuned productive behaviors since childhood. They are truly digital natives, not digital immigrants, and possibly, more fully than most, they exploit and comprehend what it means to be digitally enabled and digitally influenced. Similarly, where these individuals are ineffective (e.g., face-to-face communication) indicates a need to bring forth best practices from previous generations or to create practices to navigate new challenges of the digital world. So, please keep in mind that I'm well aware that every single thing millennials do isn't an indicator for a best approach, but it is simply outside the scope of this book to address that topic!

The behaviors discussed also lean heavily toward those individuals in jobs and careers that involve highly cognitive, nonroutine work. Some examples of this type of work include project management, customer service, and troubleshooting manufacturing issues. As we will explore in the next chapter, this is a purposeful choice because of the significant increase of nonroutine work (whether in the office or as physical labor). Routine work, even something like serving in a fast-food restaurant, is decreasing. (In the fast-food case, fully automated restaurants, complete with robots, have already been launched!) Therefore, my research has focused more heavily on reinterpreting the drivers, the needs, and behaviors of top talent, high-performing millennials in cognitive, nonroutine roles.

Many of the expectations and cultural changes in this book will resonate with modern-minded gen Z, boomers, traditionalists, and gen Xers as well; a group that we will refer to as *modern talent*. As you read this book, you may find a millennial behavior and think, "That's not just millennial! That is how I am too!" That's great! Regardless of generation, many of us have adapted well to digital technology. If you identify with a particular millennial behavior, all that means is that you identify strongly with modern perceptions of work. The caveat to keep in mind is that *for older generations, many "millennial" expectations for the workplace were wants, not needs.* Millennials and generation Z are often redefining needs—and with good reason, as I'll demonstrate in many cases.

How to Use This Book

This book focuses on transforming five of the biggest millennial stereotypes—lazy, entitled, needing to be hand-held, disloyal, and having authority issues—into more balanced strengths and, subsequently, linking them to related organizational culture changes. The focus is on providing a new language to talk about millennial behavior and thereby paving the way for more effectively addressing modern talent needs. By providing a window into each generation's perspective, the new language does something that no one has quite accomplished: close the generation gap.

In chapter 1, we begin by resetting our understanding of the millennial generation to set the stage for developing a new language. We provide a brief foundation into generational science and explain why the most common millennial stereotypes are inaccurate conclusions, especially for the broad population of top talent, cognitive-career-focused millennials. In chapters 2 through 6, we focus on developing the new language or strengths for each stereotype, as well as recommend transformations to organizational culture to harness the potential of modern talent. Finally, we close with a summary and next steps. The five stereotypes represent the most common grievances expressed by older generations and were carefully chosen through the many interviews I have conducted. The new language and related proposed organizational changes come from my experiences with millennials who are considered top talent and my emerging work with organizations to improve engagement and retention.

The stereotypes and transformations we will examine in the core chapters are as follows:

> Chapter 2: It's Not Lazy, It's Productivity Redefined

> Chapter 3: It's Not Entitled, It's Entrepreneurial

> Chapter 4: It's Not Hand-Holding, It's Agility

> Chapter 5: It's Not Disloyal, It's Seeking Purpose

> Chapter 6: It's Not Authority Issues, It's Respect Redefined

Each chapter follows a consistent structure. Using my One Coin, Two Sides model, each chapter begins with an explanation of the stereotypical behavior and interpretation of the root cause from the traditional mindset and the modern mindset. Consider that just as every coin has two sides, every millennial behavior can be interpreted multiple ways. And, of course, we each think our own interpretation is right! I have simplified the trends into two perspectives (traditional and modern) in order to create an easy-to-digest model, but there are certainly other interpretations that could be added. During this compare and contrast, through exploring the traditional perspective, we will learn how the stereotypical interpretation emerged. Then, I form the basis for the proposed new language through exploring the modern perspective.

Armed with a more balanced overall interpretation, I drive the connection to specific organizational culture changes. I follow with "Tales from the Trenches" of the organizational change in action, many of which are new and experimental initiatives. I have included stories from a variety of industries and have kept the global context in mind throughout. In addition, you will encounter stories of successful and not-so-successful millennials, boomers, gen Xers, and their cross-generational relationships. There are many boomers and gen Xers who do passionately believe in shaping the future and understanding the insights millennials bring. These are the individuals and organizations that I have highlighted in this book in the form of stories, case studies, and best practices.

The end of each chapter has two key tools to help you take action to create your modern culture. The first is a short self-assessment entitled "How Modern Is Your Culture?" The assessment allows you to do a "gut check" on how your organization is doing on the material covered in the chapter. It is an adaptation of my groundbreaking Modern Culture Diagnostic consulting solution that helps organizations identify their strengths and opportunity areas for attracting, retaining, and developing modern talent. By completing the self-assessment, you will get a feel for the maturity of your organization in meeting modern talent needs.

The second tool shifts the focus from your organization to you. The 10-Minute Champion is a brief collection of actions you can do in 10 minutes or less per day to champion modern culture. An apt metaphor for the 10-Minute Champion is a Twitter-sized approach to changing the workplace. Consider picking one item to champion from each chapter based on what you think is the easiest to implement and/or will have the greatest impact.

Finally, I have provided an invaluable online resource library to accompany the book. The library is located at themillennialmyth.com /resources and includes the following tools and resources:

> **An online version of the "How Modern Is Your Culture?" self-assessment via live survey.** You can view the results of the survey in real time and see how your responses compare with other readers.

> **One-page summary guides for each chapter.** These include links to deeper references as a convenient way for you to source data and insight for your own initiatives. This is also a great resource for professors of graduate programs who wish to use this book as a way to spark discussion about generational trends and the modern workplace.

> **Live collaboration space for capturing key insights.** Many readers often use a personal document to capture key insights as they read. To enrich this activity, the online library includes a collaboration document with quotes and key points that stood out for other readers of this book. I welcome you to add your own thoughts as you read along.

> **10-Minute Champion idea space.** Contribute your own 10-Minute Champion ideas and get more from other readers in this online collaboration document.

Although I am not a boomer or gen Xer, I have tried my best through anecdotal interviews and research to accurately represent the journey that has led to the existing perspectives shared in the traditional interpretation section of each chapter. While you may not personally agree with every perspective shared, consider it as a starting point for discussion of what you do believe or what did influence you. You may find that some people around you do share the perspectives of other generations, while some may not. That's okay! Throughout the book, the focus is not on definitively identifying each and every perspective but on asking the questions "What's changed?" and "How does that impact the workplace?" You may find additions you'd like to make to the various perspectives. Similarly, there will be millennials you have met who do not follow the patterns presented here. Any global considerations and differences are also important to note. I encourage you to be a part of our community as you embark on this journey. There are many others who have similar questions and best practices to share. Also, I encourage you to reach out to me with your thoughts.

■ ■ ■

In summary, the significant disconnect between the prevalent biases about millennials and the reality is creating inertia toward the already difficult challenge of workplace modernization. Ultimately, it is driving the struggles with attracting, engaging, and retaining talent today. This book aims to not only correct these misunderstandings and redirect the conversation on millennials, but move organizations forward in creating their unique, modern workplace culture.

People who have been there forever, left to their own devices, are rarely in the best position to design the future. It's those who consciously listen to the constituents of the future who can understand which direction to move in. It's not the captain holed up in a room with the map and ship's course who can best steer the ship. It's the helmsman, the crew member who stands out on the deck with the map, feeling the direction of the wind change and conscious of the current, who makes the ship reach its destination. We thrive when we are pulled by the future, not pushed by the past.

Jack Welch, ex-CEO of General Electric, once said, "If the rate of change on the outside exceeds the rate of change on the inside, the end is near."[7] Through this pivotal time of generation transition and digital transformation, some companies will become a Blockbuster, some a Netflix. Do I need to even ask which one you want to be?

1

Rebuilding the Backdrop for Millennials

Nothing is more damaging to a new truth than an old error.

—Johann Wolfgang von Goethe

Today's new truth is that millennials are indeed bringing positive changes to the workplace and society at large. Unfortunately, over the last decade, errors have been made in shaping the perception of this generation. As a result, the biggest danger facing the millennial generation and their potential for success is what today's dominant population, boomers and Xers, think of them.

As an example, consider an experience I had after leading a powerful panel discussion about millennials. Many audience members of older generations shared how much my message resonated with them and how they felt a new sense of clarity about millennials. However, a corporate vice president in the audience pulled me aside and said, "But really, Crystal, at the end of the day, all millennials want is money, just like everyone else. Especially when they grow up." Having just explored my own story of pursuing potential during the panel, as well as the unconventional stories of five other millennials on stage (who were all grown ups!), I was a bit taken aback. I asked, "Sir, have you talked to many millennials?" He responded, "My kids are millennials and yeah they want the new car, the new clothes, and the mansion." I thought for a moment before responding, "Well, sir, those are the kids you raised. Those aren't all the kids out there. There might even be more to your own kids than you realize."

He laughed in response and I smiled, but the conversation clearly gave him something to think about. He had bought into the stereotypical perception of the millennial generation. Consider the lens this vice president was wearing every time he looked at members of the youngest generation. How many excuses and explanations did he make to justify the exceptions he encountered among the millennial generation? How often did he refuse to make a change to create modern culture in the workplace because he felt he would be pandering to the younger generation?

In comparison, a boomer I work closely with has had a lifelong philosophy to always stay connected to "the new," the latest changes going on. One way she does this is by making sure to work with younger people. After a successful career in research and development and later training, she has retired and yet, she purposefully pursues keeping fresh. Our relationship is one where I learn from her and she learns from me, an interdependent and most importantly (in her words) *fun* relationship. She is one to experiment with and embrace new approaches. How has having this lens created opportunities for her that would otherwise have been absent? What does her ability to build relationships across generations look like? How does looking beyond the biases represented in media help her create an objective, strategic approach?

Many leaders stubbornly cling to an "it's always been done this way" mentality and, even if they want to, have limited tools to discover what modernizing means because media paints millennials as impossible overgrown children who have now joined the workplace. The tools are limited to what works at organizations thought of as sexy by millennials: Google, Amazon, Facebook, start-ups. Often, these tools simply don't make sense for other industries. As a result, the millennial generation is seen as an enormous challenge, something to be managed, to be taught, to be contended with, and ultimately, to be integrated into how we have always done things. Yet there are two sides to every story.

The Elephant in the Room: Why Lazy, Entitled, Job-Hopper Is A Useless, Inaccurate Perception

What do these negative perceptions sound like? Consider the following phrases, questions, and comments I often come across in my interactions with corporate leaders, including HR:

> ❯ They are lazy, entitled job-hoppers.

> ❯ Why do we have to pander to millennials?

> ❯ They need to be babied and hand-held.

> ❯ They want to be handed everything without putting in the work.

> ❯ We've given them more than we had and they still aren't satisfied.

> ❯ They think they can just walk into a room with the CEO and gain an audience.

> ❯ They don't have a sense of decorum.

> ❯ The millennials are the same as everyone else. They want what everyone wants.

> ❯ One day, they will have to grow up and be driven by money and the same things that everyone always has been concerned with.

These are the prevailing perceptions, spoken or unspoken, every time a young person is invited to interview, every time a new hire starts, and every time a young colleague is promoted to a management position. As Eric Hoover wrote in the *Chronicle of Higher Education*, "Such descriptions are reminders that most renderings of millennials are done by older people, looking through the windows of their own experiences."[1] These perceptions are wrong and fundamentally damaging to employee engagement, workplace productivity, and positive culture-building.

It's not enough to know the business impacts of these negative perceptions. To create a blank page for understanding millennials, we need to address the elephant in the room up front with two key arguments against today's top prevailing negative perceptions: that millennials are lazy, entitled, job-hopping, need to be hand-held, and have issues with authority.

Argument 1:
Yes, "They Have It Better and
Easier Now"—But So Do You

"When I was young, I had to walk four miles in the snow, barefoot, uphill both ways. Kids these days have it too easy." This cliché captures an important truth: every generation has complained about the generations that followed. In reality, every generation has been lazier and more entitled compared to the previous generation's idea of hard work because *every generation's goal is to make life easier for the next generation.*

Boomers may have had to share a room with another sibling or wait in line to use the house's single corded phone. In comparison, a member of the traditionalist generation may have had to share a room with their whole family or wait for a telegram to hear from a loved one. Sure, in today's generation most everyone has their own cell phone and the majority can afford housing with separate rooms for each child. But that doesn't mean millennials are any more entitled or lazy than boomers were perceived to be by traditionalists.

Everyone has benefited from innovations such as access to better health care, public utilities, and transportation. Everyone has benefited from technology and as a result, *we all have become lazier and more entitled.* Especially in first world countries, regardless of age or generation, people expect to have access to clean water, food, transportation, education, and jobs. We have reached a level of comfort such that not only are our basic needs met, but our self-actualization needs are met as well. These are all luxuries that most previous generations did not have. To blame the millennial generation for enjoying the fruits of humanity's progress since childhood is a behavior borne out of misdirected bitterness and envy—vices that serve to encumber decision making instead of empowering it.

Also, as in every other generation, just because society has made life better for people doesn't mean that new challenges haven't arisen in their place. Yes, we are instantly connected today to our loved ones via cell phones. But then again, we are instantly and always permanently connected to a world of overwhelming information. Yes, we can Google knowledge in seconds that took many people many years to accumulate. But then again, the expectations for today's new employees to be able to process all this information are much different than they were for employees of yesteryear.

In summary, in some ways we are all lazier and more entitled than the generations that preceded us. In addition, we all have had to face new challenges that preceding generations did not predict or experience. The constant societal evolution toward better is one big reason why it is a grave error to characterize an entire generation as lazy, entitled, disrespectful, hand-held job-hoppers.

Argument 2:
Stereotyping Is Discrimination and Promotes Exclusion. Period.

Consider this question: What if the words "lazy" and "entitled" were used to describe another subgroup? For example, all women are lazy and entitled. This would be considered discrimination and slanderous. Even softer versions such as "Why should we pander to [ethnic group] needs?" implies discrimination instead of inclusion. Organization leaders and employees, as always, should be careful about using discriminatory language, at a minimum to avoid legal issues.

Furthermore, it is impossible to build an inclusive culture while simultaneously projecting stereotypes. Many organizations profess a desire to create an inclusive cross-generational workplace in today's world where an unprecedented five generations are working side by side. Those same organizations, however, often knowingly and unknowingly express disrespect for millennials verbally and through behaviors.

For example, a 27-year-old millennial manager shared with me her experience with her one-up manager. The millennial had joined an organization after earning her bachelor's and master's degrees while working throughout college. She joined the organization at a managerial level and as a result, her gen X manager often comments, "You're so lucky to be getting all this responsibility at your age." Statements such as these subtly underscore the assumption that she was not deserving of her job because of her age, instead of appreciating that her strengths and experience simply fit the needs of the job. Many managers would see nothing wrong with this statement, but on the receiving end, it creates a consistent undertone of resentment.

Paul Meshanko, in his book *The Respect Effect* and related talks, shares his brilliant research on respect and its impact on productivity and engagement.[2] He writes, "Respect biologically programs and primes our brains to do our very best work. It frees the pre-frontal complex, the most productive part of the brain that does complex problem solving, prioritizing, collaborating with people, to do its best work. When I'm treated with disrespect, that part of the brain goes silent, unable to do work." To encourage a cross-generationally inclusive, productive atmosphere for modern talent, we need to deliberately and intentionally create an atmosphere of respect for all generations.

Meshanko goes on to explain the biological challenges of doing so and how to overcome them: "When we engage people with suspicion, our behaviors become distinctly unproductive. We go out of our way to avoid them. We can also become hostile, where we spend our energy hurting other people and their ability to contribute. The problem is we are suspicious by nature. How do we overcome that? We go back to a state of mind we had when we were children. Instead of being suspicious when we didn't know someone, we were curious. When we can replace suspicion with curiosity, we approach each other to understand our differences and give them context."

Reading this book, written by a millennial, is one way in which you are intentionally engaging on a journey to respectfully understand the differences and context of the millennial generation. Instead of labeling and discriminating against millennials with words like "lazy" and "entitled," you can choose to actively become curious about, instead of suspicious of, the changes in expectation and behavior millennials are bringing forward. It may be difficult, but it will help you become proud of how you handle your everyday conversations with the newest members of the workforce. By doing so, not only are you avoiding legal repercussions, you are one step closer to building an inclusive atmosphere that creates productivity, engagement, and a commitment to dignity for all in your organization.

Generational Science Applied:
The Formative Events That Defined the Millennials

In the next chapters, we will explore alternative language for the five most common millennial generation stereotypes: lazy, entitled, needing to be hand-held, disloyal, and having issues with authority. Before doing so, let's have a firm understanding of generational science and the statistics and events that influenced the millennial generation.

A generation is defined as "a cohort born in the same date range that experienced the same events during their formative years." As a result, sociologists say that some conclusions can be drawn about the cohort's attitudes, values, and beliefs, which comprises the essence of generational science.

Let's explore why the focus on formative events is important. Experiencing significant events as a child is different than experiencing events as an adult. Many people today comment that innovations like the Internet haven't just affected millennials, they've affected everyone. While that statement is true, adults have a predefined context with which to interpret significant events. Children, on the other hand, shape their context anew, for the first time, when significant events occur; this newly formed context then becomes the lens through which they interpret the world as adults.

In addition, children are significantly influenced by their parents. The behaviors and experiences parents share with their children as a result of events shape their kids' context as well. For example, in the United States, we can imagine that the widely publicized Columbine high school shooting, in which two teens killed 13 people and wounded more than 20 others before committing suicide, potentially created a parenting style that overly focused on child safety, one factor in what is commonly known as "helicopter parenting." Where once kids were allowed to roam freely, today parents keep a much tighter grip on their whereabouts. This is one of many formative events that shaped values, expectations, and beliefs differently for millennials compared to other generations.

A second component of the definition for generational science is that the conclusions drawn should aim to be about collective attitudes, values, and beliefs. To say that the millennial generation values or believes in being babied and hand-held doesn't make sense. However, to say that the millennial generation values real-time feedback is appropriate. One statement seeks to interpret the motivation behind the behavior or value, and therefore becomes a discriminatory conclusion. The other focuses on the value held and leaves discussion open for a diverse range of why.

A common mistake is to attribute traits, values, and beliefs to a generation, when instead they are a function of age, marital status, income, or other factors. For example, when considering benefits, policies, and cultural elements for boomer employees, it's much more useful to consider their life stage and the challenges of that stage (a function of age) than the formative events they experienced as children (the intention of generational studies).

Finally, let's consider the cultural component of the definition of a generation. The birth date range and name of generations are typically defined differently around the world because different events have taken place historically that shaped the distinctions between generations. However, as globalization has increased facilitated by the Internet, so has the similarity of generational definition. Hence, in the highly globalized world of today, the emergence of the millennial generation is typically considered a global phenomenon, albeit with local differences that we should account for. When referring to older generations, however, we must be even more careful not to assume similarities between nations in birth date range, names, or characteristics. Some of the stereotypes we discuss may sound like a US phenomenon at first glance, but the underlying millennial behaviors are often something many cultures are experiencing.

With a complete understanding of the word "generation" in hand, let's compare the generations today and draw some initial conclusions on the impact to the workplace.

Key Trends, Events, and Statistics

Let's consider the socioeconomic statistics and events that define the millennial generation.

Again, if you work for a global organization or are based in a different country, I encourage you to find the statistics that define the generations in your country of interest. In general, while the absolute values may differ, many of the trends for millennials may sound familiar because of the wide-reaching influence of digital technology. The statistics related to economic and societal trends, however, may differ significantly.

Here are how the generations are defined in the United States:

Table 1.1 Defining generations in the US.

Generation	Birth Year Range	Age (as of 2016)	Approximate US Population	Number of US births in this date range
Silent/ Traditionalists	1928–1945	71–88	28 Million	47 Million
Baby Boomers	1946–1964	52–70	74.9 Million	76 Million
Generation X	1965–1980	36–51	66 Million	55 Million
Millennials	1981–1996	20–35	75.4 Million	66 Million
Generation Z	1996–now	0–19	75 Million*	69 Million

*Estimated population of generation Z as of December 2015.[3]
Source: Pew Research 2015 and 2016 data sets.[4]

A generation's size often determines how it influences societal changes. Some of the factors that impact size of generation include birth rate, death rate, immigration rate, and the presence of conflicts such as war or environmental disasters. For example, the decreased birth rate demonstrates one reason why generation X is a smaller population. In addition to the increased birth rate, the high immigration rate for millennials has increased their overall population to 75.4 million, overtaking the 74.9 million boomers in 2016.[5]

In addition to the size of each generation, other societal trends have made an impact. The battles fought for ethnic and gender equality significantly progressed during the boomer generation and the results are overwhelmingly evident in the millennial generation. For example, during the boomer generation, women made significant strides into higher education and the workforce. Today, millennials are the most educated generation in terms of number of degrees earned. In addition, females are outpacing males in this arena, with 27 percent of female millennials earning at least a bachelor's degree compared to 21 percent of male millennials! That is nearly double the number of female boomers who held bachelor's degrees (14 percent).[6] In addition, the millennial Caucasian population in the US has fallen below 60 percent, compared to 77 percent during the boomer generation.[7] Companies today with primarily Caucasian, male leadership should take notice of these changes.

Millennials are also the most diverse generation in history, not just by ethnicity but by income, parent marital status, and individual marital status. Millennials experienced a wide range of parenting styles, including the continuation of single-parent homes. Though there is much debate and diversity when calculating the rate of divorce, it's agreed that it sharply increased during gen X's formative years and has fallen since then, but it remains much higher than for the boomer generation. In addition, there has been a rise in homes with remarried parents and no parents. Only 46 percent of children in 2013 lived in two-parent first-marriage homes, compared to 61 percent in 1980 and 73 percent in 1960.[8] Millennials are also delaying marriage significantly. Compared to 64 percent of the Silent generation and 49 percent of boomers, only 28 percent of millennials aged 18 to 32 are married.[9]

Lastly, inflation and recession have hit millennials hard. Underemployment and unemployment are still highest for the millennial generation compared to other generations, more than eight years after the recession. In addition, college costs have risen exponentially, from $929 per year in 1963 to $17,474 per year in 2013 for four-year public colleges

Table 1.2 Summary of generational socioeconomic trends.

	Generation				
	Silent	**Boomer**	**Gen X**	**Millennials**	**Gen Z**
% Caucasian	84%	77%	66%	57%	
% Married (at age 18–32)	64%	49%	38%	28%	
% In Two-Parent, First-Marriage Homes		73%	61%	46%	
% Bachelor's Degrees, male	12%	17%	18%	21%	
% Bachelor's Degrees, female	7%	14%	20%	27%	
Four-year Public College Tuition, Fees, and Room/Board per year (in 2015 dollars)		$929	$2,327	$8,274	$17,474

Sources: Pew Research Center, National Center for Education Statistics.[11]

(stated in 2015 dollars). For private institutions, the jump is even more drastic, from $1,810 in 1963 to $35,074 in 2013.[10] This is in sharp contrast to the relatively favorable economic prospects for boomers upon graduation, when a college degree essentially guaranteed a job and didn't require an enormous debt.

What do these societal trends indicate regarding the workplace? There are several initial conclusions we can draw from the above statistics:

> **Short-term trend (next 5 to 10 years)—accelerated leadership development of millennials.** Reviewing the population statistics, in the US, there are not enough gen Xers to fill the leadership gaps left behind by boomers. As boomers retire, gen Xers will be taking on an increased workload if millennials haven't been adequately prepared to step in. Organizations that currently lack mentoring and have unstructured training programs will find they have a hard time accelerating development compared to those that do. Gen Z will likely have a similar population size as millennials, so this particular demographic shift is specific for today's generation transition. For first world countries, this trend is generally the case. For some third world countries, often up to

50 percent of the population is composed of those under the age of 25 and therefore, there are differing challenges.

> **Mid-term trend (next 30 years)—job-hopping due to lack of trust in organizations.** Instead of preparing for a midlife crisis, millennials often intend to have a quarter-life crisis. For many, this is a direct result of witnessing higher divorce rates and parents who have experienced layoffs, benefit reductions, and regrets about putting their eggs in one, usually unfulfilling, basket during the Great Recession. Millennials are spending more time in their early career years exploring self and their passions. Delaying marriage also allows for pursuing careers for exploration instead of "for the paycheck." Organizations that help them discover and leverage their strengths and passions, while having a clear commitment to valuing employees, have a distinct advantage with talent that has witnessed the recession. Gen Z has been affected similarly. If the global economy continues to recover and trust is rebuilt, this trend could be partially reversed.

> **Long-term trend (beyond 30 years)—engaging a highly diverse population.** It is very difficult to characterize millennials in the workplace because of their much greater diversity than previous generations, including their gender, ethnicity, income background, and parenting style. With more than half of the college graduates being female and only 60 percent being Caucasian, we can expect a wider variety of expectations. Because of this diversity, the common attributes of "everyone gets a trophy" or being reared by "helicopter parents" don't necessarily ring true across the full generation. Eric Hoover was pointed in his criticism of the generational labels: "Over the last decade, commentators have tended to slap the millennial label on white, affluent teenagers who accomplish great things as they grow up in the suburbs, who confront anxiety when applying to super-selective colleges, and who multi-task with ease as their helicopter parents hover reassuringly above them. The label tends not to appear in

renderings of teenagers who happen to be minorities or poor, or who never won a spelling bee."[12] Similarly, gen Z and generations to come will have greater diversity, especially with increasing globalization. Modern talent is diverse and expects diversity to be present and respected in the workplace.

A Bird's-Eye View on the Impact of Technology

In addition to the socioeconomic reasons, the way we work, study, and live has also been dramatically changed by the evolution of the computer, the Internet, social media, and mobile devices. Understandably, the tools millennials grew up using in school have translated to expectations of the workplace.

Consider the following trends. As you review, if you are a non-millennial, consider the world you grew up in instead and how the messages and tools you had exposure to may have been different.

> **What children can learn has changed drastically.** It's an undeniable fact that young people have access to greater amounts of information via the Internet and have the opportunity to learn more than previous generations did at the same age. As much as we often hate to admit it, people graduating today have a lot more knowledge in topics that are relevant today than they are given credit for. High school students, for example, participate on robotics teams instead of playing outside with no rules. As stated before, however, with any innovation, some skills are gained, some are transformed, and some are lost. Kids today may not learn at all about some skills that are considered basic knowledge by previous generations.

> **Children can gain respect through sharing their voice.** Regardless of age, everyone is able to contribute their voice to the Internet and gain a following. The Internet is the great equalizer. Teens have a greater entrepreneurial spirit, desire to pursue potential, and a different skill set than graduates of previous

generations as a result of their exposure to digital technology and the Internet.

> **The type of work done in organizations has changed.** For the general employee base, the type of jobs available has shifted drastically from routine manual (10 percent loss since 2001) and routine cognitive (8 percent loss) to nonroutine cognitive (+24 percent growth) and nonroutine manual (+32 percent growth).[13] Furthermore, the days of the intern making copies and bringing coffee are disappearing rapidly. New employees are expected to become contributors rapidly as a result of today's VUCA (volatile, uncertain, complex, ambiguous) business environment. This change is a key contributor to this book's focus on top talent millennials who work in highly cognitive, nonroutine roles.

> **The way workers communicate and interact has changed.** The ability to work virtually and impact across global boundaries has exponentially increased. The amount of time spent outdoors and/or face-to-face has decreased. Relationship and communication skills are shifting. Kids today have grown up contributing to social campaigns to help other countries during times of

Figure 1.1 Employment in routine vs. nonroutine jobs has diverged since 2001[14]

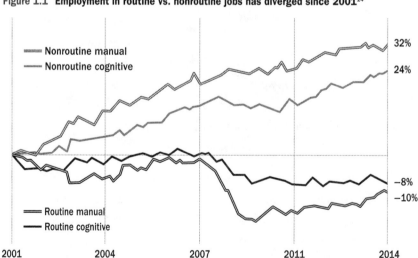

need. They are often more comfortable communicating behind a screen than in person.

In summary, the millennial generation is exquisitely diverse, exposed to more information at younger ages than previous generations and dealing with new-to-the-world obstacles, because of the technological and social changes present in their formative years. They are a reflection of a wide variety of parenting styles, backgrounds, education systems, world events, and innovations. They are a living, breathing example of how the groundbreaking innovations of the last 50 years have impacted and will continue to impact society. These rapid changes explain why the gap between generations today is so wide, in the US and even more so in third world countries. Some of the approaches millennials use are important signs of changes to the status quo; some are signs of what we risk losing if we aren't careful. They allow us to question and reexamine our assumptions for how we work and live today. When millennial workplace expectations are considered inappropriate, are leaders and managers taking into account a well-rounded perspective on the impact of these socioeconomic and technological changes?

Older generation leaders who successfully understand millennials often are motivated by highly personal reasons. One such champion I encountered had experienced a tragedy with the death of her teenage son. During this time, she experienced a wide amount of support from her son's friends, who created fund-raisers and nonprofit efforts in her son's name using social media. Since that time, she has never agreed with the stereotypes about millennials. In another instance, Lee, an "on the cusp" gen X/boomer, spent a great deal of time with his daughter's rowing team as their unofficial photographer. He witnessed such high collaboration, dedication, and perseverance, it was forever imprinted in his mind that this generation is yet another great generation. He wanted to support the generation in any way he could, especially in light of the overall perception. Once a stranger to me, he reached out to find opportunities for me to help spread the belief he felt so strongly about. In these very personal moments of transformation, one gains a sense of appreciation of being in the others' shoes. What have we learned from successful cross-generational relationships? Consider the power these individuals have discovered by integrating our different lenses into a more complete view.

■ ■ ■

At this point, we should be grounded in why this is an important topic for business, why lazy and entitled are ineffective conclusions, what the definition of a generation is, and the big picture of socioeconomic and innovation trends that have impacted the various generations. Now we are ready to explore the five most common stereotypes in detail and what they really tell us about the modern workplace instead. Through the thought processes, stories, and best practices presented, reflect on your ability to speak a new language and consider what actions you will take as a modern workplace champion.

It's Not Lazy, It's
Productivity Redefined

*When I see a gen Y concentrating on their smartphone, my first
thought used to be that they were playing video games or conversing
with friends. Knowing now that technology plays a larger role
in a gen Y's life than my own boomer life, I recognize that such
technology helps a gen Y participate and communicate at work.*

—Post-Program Learnings, participant in Invati Consulting's
Generation University training program

A millennial employee arrives to work at half past nine, plugs in some
headphones, and stays at their desk until five thirty, eating snacks and
lunch along the way. A boomer arrives at eight, proceeds to alternate
desk time with conversations to complete various tasks, and leaves at six.
A gen Xer arrives at seven, rushes from meeting to meeting, and leaves at
three thirty to pick up their child from school. How do we know which
one is working hardest?

Let's consider the definitions of hard work and laziness. The *Oxford
Dictionary* defines laziness as "the quality of being unwilling to work or
use energy." Hardworking is defined as "tending to work with energy and
commitment." Whether it is the farmer working from sunup to sundown
or the manager darting from one meeting to the next, it can be argued
that each is doing hard work. Notably, neither definition says anything

about the goal of the work or the process used to complete work. Both definitions position hard work and laziness as subjective qualities. There is clearly room for interpretation.

How have we been interpreting the work and work ethic of millennials? Is our interpretation correct? Has the perceived definition of work always stayed the same? If the word "lazy" doesn't describe millennial behavior, what does?

One Coin, Two Sides Model: Lazy or Redefining Productivity?

Let's use the One Coin, Two Sides model to explore the behavior of millennials. Recall that in this model, we look at how observable behaviors can be interpreted through the eyes of a traditional perspective in comparison to a millennial-based modern perspective. Keep in mind that not every older person has a traditional mindset. There are many forward thinkers and many traditional thinkers, across all age spans and generations. What we are referring to here is a particular perspective or mindset that's not necessarily defined by age.

For this particular stereotype, the observable behavior is that millennials desire to work when and where they want. From a traditional perspective, this can be perceived as lazy because their beliefs are based in a world where putting in structured time equals work coming out. In contrast, from a modern, top talent perspective, this flexible work style is borne out of redefining what it takes to accomplish work today. Table 2.1 summarizes the observable behavior, the two sides, and the supporting beliefs.

Exploring the Traditional Interpretation: Lazy

Let's dive a little bit deeper into how the observable behavior of millennials causes the perception of laziness. Millennials are perceived as lazy when they:

> Request nonstandard work hours

> Don't want to come in to the office to complete their work

Table 2.1

One Coin: One Observable Behavior	
Desire to work when and where one wants, including struggling to commit to working for a set duration, within set hours, in a set location.	
Side 1: Traditional Interpretation Lazy; unwilling to put in the time	**Side 2: Top Talent, Millennial-Based Modern Interpretation** Seeking to redefine productivity
Supporting Beliefs: ❯ Putting in the time gets the work done. ❯ If I physically see someone present, I feel more assured that they are working. ❯ If someone is not putting in the time at the schedule expected, their performance may be compromised. ❯ A worker should conform to productivity standards defined by the organization.	**Supporting Beliefs:** ❯ Putting in the time and achieving work goals are separate actions and in today's world often mutually exclusive. Those who put in the time may in fact be less productive than those who focus on doing what is needed to achieve the work goal. ❯ I should be able to decide what is most productive for me and work together with my organization to align with the business and team's needs

Source: Invati Consulting

> Are on their device, "distracted from doing real work"

> Attempt to turn a hobby into a business instead of working a traditional 9 to 5 job where one is forced to "put in the time." Starting a business is often seen as a ploy to avoid the "real world" and "growing up."

From a traditional perspective, because millennials desire to work when, where, and how they want and feel okay asking to work outside the normal structure, they are perceived to be lazy. Yet recall the definitions of hard work and laziness do not prescribe how the work gets done, but only remark on whether one is willing to put in energy.

The long-standing perception of "hard work" has been based on an assumption that if you are putting in time, you are putting in effort, and that effort leads to productivity. While that conclusion made sense in yesteryear, it does not hold true in many cases today. How did we arrive at this perception of hard work? Here is a high-level overview of the evolution of work structure.

Prior to mass manufacturing, in the so-called Agrarian Age, the most common job was in a particular trade or in farming. During this time, the primary goal was to produce goods to become self-sufficient, which was difficult to do. Basic needs often weren't met, except for a handful of wealthy elite. Working from sunup to sundown was the norm. Work was seasonal and measurable. Tasks took a certain amount of time, had to be done within a certain amount of time, and results could be easily measured. The challenges to productivity were weather- or socioeconomic-related, such as drought, war, famine, or disease.

As mechanization and factories emerged, society evolved into what is commonly called the Industrial Age. Initially, the same schedule was pursued. People, including children, worked 12 to 16 hours per day. Self-sufficiency was still the primary goal. However, although factory work could be just as routine as fieldwork, if not more so, workers faced dangerous work conditions and unpredictable layoffs. Unions fought for workers' rights such as a regular, reduced workday in order to improve worker quality of life.

In the early 1900s, the workplace reached a turning point with Henry Ford and his new assembly line approach to manufacturing cars. Ford was among the first to cut back the workday to eight hours. Notably, he also doubled his workers' wages. When Ford's profit in turn doubled that of his competitors, other organizations started to get onboard. The eight-hour workday was a fight that took place over a hundred years and, surprisingly, is a relatively new concept. Federally, the law that instituted the eight-hour workday, 40-hour workweek, wasn't passed until 1937.

At this time, productivity was again defined by physical units produced, which could be directly tied to time. The basic goal of mass manufacturing was to produce units in an efficient manner with the least amount of skill required. Every individual had a manual, often repetitive, relatively easy-to-do task where the time put in could directly be linked to the number of units produced. Output had a measurable quality or result tied to it.

In the last 40 years, concepts such as Six Sigma and lean manufacturing, based on analyzing time spent, money invested, and revenue generated for each workplace activity, have been the leading models for a productive workplace. The idea of "9 to 5" is strongly based in the manufacturing mindset and is actually a vast improvement from generations past. Based on this mindset, the unsurprising perception is that if you don't want to work the (better) hours and at the location your employer has set, you don't want to work. And that appears to be the very definition of lazy: an unwillingness to work or use energy.

However, this mindset has many dangers. I once had a manager who sent out an invite at 6:00 A.M. for a meeting at 8:00 A.M. on the same day. Many employees carpooled to work, myself included, and it made it impossible for me to arrive on time. After arriving 10 minutes late and attending the meeting, I was called into the manager's office to talk about my performance issues and lack of prioritization, with the morning's meeting as the prime example. This might sound unusual, but it is a commonplace experience for many: managers and even coworkers judge other people's performance based on their arrival and departure times. And yet, the idea that a correlation exists between time and performance is far from a hard-stated fact for the type of work we most often do today.

The overarching beliefs of the traditional mindset are that putting in the time means getting the work done and that the organization defines what is most productive for employees. Consider, however, do we still live in a manufacturing world today? What other beliefs or societal norms do you feel influence the perception of laziness? How much has genuinely changed in the last 20 years that has affected the beliefs of the youngest adults in the workforce? If the only labor you have ever seen is labor done behind a computer, do you still believe in the same models for a productive workplace? What productivity do we stand to gain by testing the assumptions of 9 to 5?

Exploring the Modern Interpretation: Redefining Productivity

After World War II, there was a significant increase in people going to college, because of postwar benefits that funded higher education for veterans. Inventions such as radio and television gave birth to business-related fields like mass-scale marketing and advertising and with that an increased need for knowledge workers. The knowledge worker's job was not to produce units. More and more, it was to manage work, be creative, think strategically, provide services, and build relationships. Success in these tasks slowly became more and more unrelated to the time put in.

With the emergence of digital technology in the last 30 years, we have passed the tipping point. Most jobs for the well educated are based on knowledge or nonroutine manual instead of routine manual labor. As mentioned previously, routine manual jobs have declined 10 percent, while cognitive jobs have increased by over 30 percent in the last decade.[1]

In addition, we are quickly moving toward higher cognitive levels as lower-level knowledge tasks become automated due to technology. While we are aware of manufacturing and factory jobs being replaced by automated machinery and robots as well as being moved overseas to cheaper labor economies, what's new is that now office jobs are up for automation due to increasingly intelligent software. According to an extensive research study done by Oxford's Department of Engineering Science, 47 percent of the labor force has a high probability of becoming supplanted by automation.[2] This includes long-standing career paths such as bookkeeping and financial advising. The remaining 53 percent of jobs are less at risk because they require a higher order of human thinking, intuition, and skill.

What does all this have to do with flexible work styles? Although every technological revolution has come with the same fear of unemployment, the reality is that labor moves to new places, new skills, and new career paths. *In the highly cognitive, complex skills world that we are moving into, I'd like to posit that 9 to 5 is not likely to be the most productive work structure.* To succeed in this new world, we need to proactively consider what work structure is going to win in the future of automation and cognitive, nonroutine jobs where skilled workers will be in demand.

In addition to the evolution of highly cognitive jobs, another big difference between generations is the societal evolution of gender equality, not just in the workplace but at home. This evolution is another driver for higher work-life flexibility expectations. The 2015 Ernst & Young survey *Global Generations: A Global Study on Work-Life Challenges* reported that only 47 percent of working boomers have a full-time working spouse, compared to 73 percent of gen Xers and 78 percent of millennials.[3] This means that *less than one out of every two boomers* understand the challenges and necessity of a dual-income household in today's environment. And the empathy gap only gets worse when millennials start their family: 26 percent reported having their number of working hours increase compared to 16 percent of boomers, yet new millennial parents are half as likely to leave their job as boomers were when they had children.

For older generations, it may also come as a surprise that today only 35 percent of employed millennial men without children believe that men should be breadwinners and women should be caregivers. According to a *Washington Post* review of the EY study, "Nearly 40 percent of young workers, male or female, in the United States are so unhappy with the lack of paid parental-leave policies that they say they would be willing to move to another country."[4] While few may take this extreme action, the message is clear: workplace policies are needed that support egalitarian relationships. Millennial men want equivalent parental leave policies and millennial women want to share household responsibilities while pursuing an ambitious career. Neither wants to be negatively impacted for their egalitarian goals, but corporate workplace policies are severely lagging in this regard.

As an example, in the engineering part of my career, I recall a work environment where I was the only female in a building of over 50 people, other than the purchasing representative and the receptionist. My manager and colleagues' ability to relate to me were next to nil—for most of them, the only women they interacted with were their wives, mothers, and sisters, many of whom worked in traditionally gender-prescribed roles such as nurses, teachers, or administrators, if they worked at all. Exploring new ideas in which employees want gender-equivalent work-life benefits was like talking about embracing an alien species. To sum it up, Karyn Twaronite, EY's global diversity and inclusion officer, said it best: "I really see that there's an empathy gap in the workplace. When there's frustration about work-life balance in the workplace, and you think your boss doesn't get it, that very likely could be true."[5] The positive results we stand to gain by creating egalitarian flexible work policies is a key element of the modern workplace—a place where employees can bring their full selves to work, while reducing stress and distractions.

In summary, considering the added work-life burden and higher cognitive load for even entry-level jobs, a new definition of productivity has evolved for millennials and modern talent. What some traditionally see as work during a standard 9 to 5 day—going from often ineffective meeting to meeting, catching up with a colleague at the watercooler, walking to another person's desk to ask a question, staying later than the boss, sacrificing personal health and relationships for work—millennials often see as a waste of time, because this traditional idea of work may not be linked to productivity. *Ironically, the old idea of work is perceived as "superficial" productivity—tasks that on the surface look like you're doing work, but in reality aren't linked to producing results.*

Instead, digitally enabled millennials, who have succeeded through school and work experiences in this information-overloaded world, see taking breaks as a part of productivity. They see minimizing stress and distractions as a part of productivity. They see working out, getting enough sleep, and eating healthy as a part of productivity. From this vantage point, desiring flexibility is not a sign of laziness, it is a sign of understanding intuitively that the future of work lies in a digital, high-cognitive-load, more egalitarian world and that flexibility is what it takes to be successful in that world. For those with the modern talent mindset, we believe that the way work has traditionally been done may in fact do more harm than good and that we should be able to have more of a say in what is most productive.

■ ■ ■

Using the One Coin, Two Sides model, we have analyzed the environment, motivations, and barriers that are driving the new behavior of modern talent. In doing so, we have now introduced the clues to design a better workplace. As we see it, neither the traditional interpretation or the modern interpretation of recent events is right or wrong. You may have additions or changes you would make to the interpretations. Again, that is okay! They are simply different, evolving ways of life—truly two sides of one coin, with room for additional interpretation. When it comes to desiring flexibility, the type of work we do has changed and the type of life we are leading has changed. However, the perceived definition of productivity, and therefore the org structure and processes, haven't quite changed. What are the modern levers we can pull for a more productive workplace?

Leveraging the New Definition of Productivity to Build Modern Organizations

Let's introduce a more detailed, goal-oriented concept of what enables modern productivity:

> *to industriously, diligently pursue tactics that allow the optimal conditions for an individual to complete the mental and physical tasks needed to deliver the company's strategic goals*

As demonstrated by the One Coin, Two Sides model, the concept of what enables productivity evolves over time. Today, we are no longer responsible for creating widgets that take predictable amounts of time, which defined productivity of yesteryear. Instead, we are charged with being creative, innovative, and strategic—all while balancing a nearly impossible home life influenced by egalitarian needs, recession, and inflation. As a result, focusing on results—what the goal is—rather than how, when, and where it gets done, takes on greater importance. The key to generating productivity in the new paradigm is to shift from "putting in the time" to "meeting goals" by enabling workplace flexibility in three areas: work hours, work environment, and access to resources. These three interventions work together to stop employees from burning out from digital work and instead maximize productivity.

First, shift the focus from strict 9 to 5 work hours to a flexible structure that still gets the work done and promotes teamwork. The objective is not to lose all workplace structure, but to allow people to operate during the hours that best work for their unique life situations

41

and neurology. Both of these aspects are equally important. If one is caring for aging parents or has children, and certain work times are more convenient, it is better to allow for those times than to have a distracted, stressed-out employee. From a neurological perspective, it may be better to have shorter stints of working on a computer with breaks that involve outdoor meetings or a period of complete disconnect from work. We need to be able "to be" as much as we need "to do" to be productive at work today!

Second, provide a mix of open office or cubicle layouts, collaborative spaces, "library"-style spaces, and outdoor areas as work environments. One of the biggest mistakes today is to eschew comprehensive understanding of all the levers available for engagement and productivity and simply invest in 100 percent open office spaces. Often, this comes from a desire to do what's "quick and dirty" and copy the superficial changes we see working at other companies. Open office is one of these trends, implemented without having a deeper understanding of the tapestry of changes that must take place in order for all changes to succeed. Studies have now emerged supporting the ineffectiveness of this approach. A study from the *Journal of Environmental Psychology* in 2013 indicated that 50 percent of workers in open-plan spaces suffer from a lack of sound privacy, and 30 percent complain about a lack of visual privacy.[6] Instead, providing a mix of spaces is much more effective to engage and enable productivity.

Lastly, productivity is determined today by how well one is able to sort and filter through vast amounts of data. Organizations aligned with technology that provide searchable, instantaneous connections to the right data, relationship, or training eliminate hours of wasted time. Traditional thinkers often complain that modern talent isn't interested in "putting in the time" to do the grunt work. But to modern talent, grunt work often looks like wading through bureaucracy and having to have the right relationships to get the right information. When putting in time is related to gaining experience, it is invaluable. When putting in the time means reinventing the wheel or becoming a member of the "old boys' club," it is wasted. Flexible methods to deal effectively with information overload are critical. These methods include everything from being able to find the right person at the right time to having spaces to take a break or allow creative inspiration to strike. We will talk more about this expectation in chapter 4.

It can be incredibly rewarding to the company and the employee to adopt a flexible approach with a goal-oriented instead of time- or location-oriented focus on performance. I had just recently relocated to a new state with my company when I discovered my passion shift from engineering to something people-related. I was on the verge of leaving the company when I came across a role in training, based in the location I had just left! Upon contacting Rick Kramer, the engineering training director at the time, we talked about the opportunity and the possibility of making it location-free. Rick was open to the idea and we discussed how it would work, including structural elements like virtual core work hours, weekly check-in meetings, and monthly visits. A month later, because of Rick's faith in being able to make it work, I transitioned into the role.

My key responsibility was to reinvent a technical training school for new hires and make it globally standard (something that had never been achieved before). It was a highly cognitive role. I worked with my teammates and gained sponsorship for my efforts virtually. I also became a first-time manager in this role and managed my new direct report virtually. And yet, my productivity increased significantly during this time. I stopped having to go to meeting after meeting or having people drop by and interrupt my flow of thought. I could choose which meetings to attend, creating clear agendas and focused working sessions. I could pause and take a walk around the neighborhood, which gave me mental capacity to create new ideas and overcome barriers. I was more intentional about building relationships and spent my time more purposefully when on-site. Ultimately, it gave me, as a millennial, the freedom to work as I always had worked before having a corporate job: outside of a cubicle, with focused, isolated time for deep thinking, with healthy breaks, and through more fun, purposeful relationships I had more choice in building.

I stayed at the company for an additional three years, making some of the best contributions I had ever made. Without Rick's openness in considering other ways of working and goal-oriented focus for performance, the company would have lost a one-rated, top talent employee years earlier than needed, and it wouldn't have gained the results of the high-performance work I delivered. I wouldn't have gained the satisfaction of a job well done, without having to undergo a disruptive relocation. We were able to merge our approaches because of our openness to other ways of doing things, resulting in a relationship that worked.

In order for a workplace to become more flexible in terms of hours, environment, and resources, the underlying attitude companies and leaders must develop is *to have more trust in their employees*. That means believing that top talent genuinely wants to meet their goals and that one does not need to be micromanaged to do so. Micromanaging may, in fact, decrease employees' abilities to meet their goals. We must build respect through approaching diverse work styles with curiosity. Who knows—in collaborating together and combining approaches, we may create some brand new, highly productive, engaging ways of working!

Tales from the Trenches

Here are some examples of initiatives from a snapshot of organizations that are pushing the boundaries and leading what modern workplace culture looks like today. Some of these are works in progress; others have seen significant results already. I have highlighted the mindset and work process that have enabled forward progress in order to help you gain insight into how to build momentum within your organization.

Case Study 2.1

Work Hour Experimentation in the Public Sector

One of the arenas where we don't often expect cutting-edge modernization is the public sector. Yet a previous governor of Utah, Jon Huntsman, pioneered a tremendous change in work-life balance in 2008. He instituted a statewide four-day workweek for all public-sector workers. When everyone else was reeling from the recession, Governor Huntsman pursued a new approach with the following implementation goals:

❖ Save money by closing public buildings an extra day

❖ Roll out new policy within one month

❖ Explore the impact on productivity, engagement, and customer satisfaction as a result of the new policy

As reported by the *Guardian*, after a year of the new policy, the results were outstanding. "Eight out of ten employees liked the four-day week and wanted it to continue. Nearly two-thirds said it made them more productive and many said it reduced conflict at home and work. Only 3 percent said it made childcare harder. Workplaces across the state reported higher staff morale and lower absenteeism. There were other surprises, too. One in three among the public thought the new arrangements actually improved access to services. Falling energy prices reduced the expected economies, but the change still saved the state millions. Staff wellbeing went up with the longer weekend and with shorter, easier commuting outside the normal rush hour, which benefited other commuters, too, by reducing congestion. It wasn't the objective, but at a stroke the four-day week cut carbon emissions by 14%."[7]

The benefits for Utah's public sector were astounding—all from changing a single organizational lever, work hours. Implementing a completely flexible work hour structure clearly would not work for the public sector. The type of work done does not allow that. However, Huntsman experimented with pushing the boundaries of 9 to 5, while saving dollars that actually allowed Utah's economy to flourish and recover quicker from the recession than other states.

Now let's explore what happens when a work environment is intentionally designed to enable productivity and positive culture.

Case Study 2.2

Diverse Work Environments to Fuel Productivity

Leveraging top talent through workplace design does not have to be a black-and-white choice between high-walled cubicles and 100 percent open office. A great example of this is Microsoft's new space in Redmond, Washington. Instead of copying and pasting the hot trend of open office, Microsoft committed resources to researching and developing a vision that would work for their community. The end result is twofold. First, productivity is higher because employees can pick and choose from a diverse range of work environments to enable their work needs in the moment. Second, the environment instantly resonates as "that's Microsoft" among new recruits and existing employees, instead of feeling like a copy-and-paste start-up environment.

Since 1999, Microsoft has invested in full-time designers to support creating the right workspaces. Today, they have nine full-time employees devoted to this goal, plus workplace strategy partners around the globe. Martha Clarkson, the first full-timer, shared highlights of the process that supported Microsoft's success:

✤ **Partnered with champions in leadership, with the business goals as the focal point.** For initiatives, the design team brings together high-level champions—vice presidents, division leaders, and even C-suite members—who realize that workspaces can enable productivity. The design team then starts with the most essential question: What are the business goals you are trying to achieve in this workspace? The design starts from the business need.

✤ **Developed a design language.** As Clarkson puts it, "When you walk into a Starbucks, you know it's a Starbucks. You don't know it from the logo on the wall, you know it from how the place feels." Although initially that may sound intangible, it's actually a very visceral, tangible experience that can be identified through research with the workforce. In Microsoft's case, all of its buildings share baseline and signature components that reflect an innovative, relevant company that is more mature than a start-up, including elements like "timeless with distinction," "elevating the ordinary," and "alone but together."[8]

❖ **Delved deeply into how people work.** In addition to consistent and engaging design across environments, Clarkson and her team deeply researched how people work through focus groups and observations. The most important considerations they found were team size, flexibility to grow or shrink as needed, and supporting the need for private, focused work, as well as collaboration. They focused heavily on choices that are functional—instead of slides and ping-pong tables, an atrium, for example, starts as energetic collaboration space and, as you ascend, evolves into quieter and more individual choices for work. In the team's research, they've found there's a reason people like working in coffee shops: "You get a chance to be a part of the community, but you don't know anyone, you're on the edge of the fray. So, we honed that concept—we focus on providing levels of aloneness," says Clarkson.

At the center of all their design methods is choice. Designs that offer people choices for their mood, the kind of work they are doing, their work style, allowing employees to leverage their own personal productivity habits. The intentional design also facilitates relationships, further increasing productivity. Employees and executives work together and a "neighborhood" approach has actually decreased the number of e-mails by encouraging conversation.[9]

Microsoft started as the quintessential tech industry workplace: fluorescent lighting, monotonous environments closed from conversation, siloed individual department goals designing the next new technology invention. Today, Microsoft has added their own unique reality back into virtual, digital work. They are a great example of a company redefining what the name "Microsoft" means to individuals—all while remaining at the forefront of designing workspaces that enable modern productivity in a healthy environment.

Case Study 2.3

(Re)Designing the Work Structure to Enable Goals

A client I worked with in the consulting industry had the ingrained notion, like many, that millennials are lazy and don't want to put in the time because of their desire for flexible (not less, mind you) working hours. Specifically, the requests interfered with the traditional mindset of billable hours *and crucially, when looking at the data, came from both millennials and gen X employees*. The focus on billable hours had enormous impact:

- ❖ **Increased turnover.** The firm was witnessing an unusually high annual turnover of 10 percent, with 58 percent of the departing employees composed of the millennial generation. The influence on generation X was also evident as 70 percent of those who left the company had been there less than five years, regardless of generation.

- ❖ **Lack of training.** The company was selective on training employees, including new talent, because that would not be able to be considered a billable hour.

- ❖ **Hiring gaps.** As a result, they were focused on hiring only experienced workers, decreasing the size of their available talent pool. Finding these workers entailed attracting top talent gen Xers, who are in limited supply considering the demographic data on gen X population size.

- ❖ **Disparity and favoritism.** They only recently started allowing work from home—and not across the board, but up to manager discretion.

This is a great example of the self-sabotage the traditional mindset can create in a modern world! As a consulting firm, the only type of workers are highly cognitive knowledge workers. What if we returned to asking why the status quo exists? Consider questions like:

- ❖ Is the only way to measure results the number of hours that are put in?

- ❖ How does time-based performance relate to the results expected by the client?

❖ What risks are present because as an organization the freedom to develop existing talent isn't available?

❖ How is productivity and profitability suffering because of the commitment to time-based performance (in this case, in the form of billable hours)?

Essentially, the consulting firm has hired brilliant college graduates only to tie their hands: creativity and problem-solving skills are curtailed by hours put in on a rigid schedule and location for where the work is done.

Although they haven't taken action yet, a possible solution would be to consider billing based on a percentage of the money they were saving or increasing for the client. In this way, consultants are incentivized to use their creativity and problem-solving skills they were hired for to maximize the solution for the client. In addition to potentially increased profits, this solution would enable modern workplace productivity in an environment composed of top talent. This is a clear example of work whose success does not depend on where and when the work is being done. Pushing the boundaries and experimenting with alternative work structures in this industry is imperative!

With these three case studies, we learn a few ways we can experiment with the new idea of enabling productivity and how others have implemented changes to move from a time- and location-oriented to goal-oriented focus for performance. Altering work hours, environment, and access to resources can be powerful levers to increase productivity and engagement, when combined with research and understanding of your top talent, unique workplace culture, and business needs.

Summary: From Lazy to Evolving Workplace Flexibility for Today's Work

In this chapter, we explored our first millennial behavior and its connection to organizational culture changes. We learned that the traditional perception of working hard resides in a more structured world, where a different type of work, and therefore different measures of good work, prevailed. Although millennials could be perceived as lazy while looking through the traditional lens, the more useful, modern perception is that millennials have responded intuitively to the changes that have occurred in the way we work, what we work on, and the goals of the work. For today's highly cognitive, nonroutine jobs and egalitarian world, workplace flexibility, not rigidity, is the key to increasing productivity. What additional perspectives would you add from your experience to the perspectives explored in the One Coin, Two Sides model?

Once we redefined what enables productivity today, we learned that workplace flexibility means flexible work hours, a flexible work environment, and access to resources. We shared stories of older generations whose traditional perspectives created barriers, like the manager with a time-focus trap he would set for employees and the workplace without a concept of egalitarian personal relationships. We also shared a story of those who leverage modern behavior like Rick and his collaborative effort to make location-free work, demonstrating the power of wearing different lenses and increasing retention, engagement, and productivity. We shared examples of successful initiatives through the story of Utah's public sector and its flexible work hours and Microsoft's workspace design. Finally, we shared a future vision to shift from time-based performance to goal-based performance in the consulting industry.

What inspired you through these stories? What ideas were sparked? By experimenting with workplace flexibility, we create possibilities to increase engagement and productivity, not just for millennials but all generations who know that in today's world, their best work may not happen between the hours of 9 to 5 in an open office or cubicle. So the next time a millennial is accused of being lazy, champion a new language! Put on a modern lens, demonstrate trust and respect for all generations, and change the conversation toward reassessing productivity.

How Modern Is Your Culture?

How well do you think your organization is meeting modern talent needs? Read each statement and place an X in the appropriate column, then sum up your score. We have stated "my company" for the focus of each statement, but feel free to replace with "my immediate work group" or another community if it serves your purpose better. The assessment can also be found online at themillennialmyth.com/resources, where you can compare your answers with other readers.

	Strongly Disagree	Disagree	Neutral	Agree	Strongly Agree
My company has defined a clear idea of the minimum structure (hours, location) needed to deliver the goals of my role.					
My company encourages people to work at the time and place that works best for their personal productivity.					
My company does a good job of defining what the desired results are and what they look like, instead of focusing on how the work gets done.					
People are rarely micromanaged at my company.					
My company provides a variety of work environments to choose that enable the task at hand.					
Total number of X's in each column:					

If the majority of your X's fall in the strongly disagree or disagree columns, your organization is leaning toward a traditional perspective that is at risk of disengaging modern talent. You may want to see where you can make some changes through reviewing portions of this chapter, trying the 10-Minute Champion ideas below, investigating our online resources, or reaching out to us for further help.

10-Minute Champion

What can you do to shift your organization toward a modern culture? Consider championing the following ideas in your work group, intended to take no more than 10 minutes each.

- ☐ **Create your personal productivity guide.** Create a personal productivity worksheet that states your preferred times and places for meetings, focused work, or other categories that are important to you. Openly highlight personal life values that influence your worksheet—for example, being there for your children or, for an introvert, having enough alone time. Take a few minutes to jot down some notes on a document—pretty formatting is not necessary! Share with your team and those you work with most closely.

- ☐ **Implement digital productivity interventions:** Become experimental! Before starting a task, consider whether it is (1) a strategic, highly cognitive task (like creating a plan), (2) a brief task (like knocking out e-mails), or (3) a group task. Quickly try a new intervention to enable productivity for the task. For example, turn off your Wi-Fi connection when you need to focus in-depth on reading or writing or thinking for a project. Another example could be taking a walk outside with a colleague instead of meeting in a room. Share your intervention with others, especially if it worked!

- ☐ **Become goal-oriented during team projects.** Before starting your next team meeting or project, take a few minutes to get crystal clear on what you want to achieve, regardless whether you are leading the meeting or project. Take an additional few minutes at the beginning of the meeting to describe your goal with clarity. Leave yourself open to how it will get done—you may have your plans, but others may have new methods to introduce as well.

- ☐ **Create your own idea.** Feel free to create your own idea to improve workplace flexibility and redefine productivity.

3

It's Not Entitled, It's Entrepreneurial

Now more than ever, young people are realizing that the future is theirs to create, not something that will simply happen to them.

—Stacy Ferreira and Jared Kleinhart, *2 Billion Under 20*[1]

Evan began reviewing toys on his YouTube channel called EvanTube when he was five. At 9 years old, he now has more than 2.8 million sub-scribers and rakes in a cool $1.3 million annually for his work.[2] Seven-year-old Alina Morse wanted a lollipop that didn't cause tooth decay. After speaking with her dentist, she invented Zollipops using $7,500 in money given to her by her grandparents, which became the only candy served at the White House on Easter in 2016. Sales have been up 378 per-cent year on year and she is now 10 years old.[3] Moziah Bridges started a bow tie company when he was 9 and became the youngest entrepreneur to participate on *Shark Tank*. In 2015, he earned $250,000 in revenue and the business continues to grow.[4]

When Evan, Alina, or Moziah turns 22, will traditional companies have what it takes to attract and retain them? The expectations of some-one who has run a business since the age of 9 are vastly different than the simple college graduate of yesteryear. While other generations also had youthful entrepreneurs, the barriers to starting a business have greatly decreased with the rise of digital technology. Entrepreneurship is not necessarily defined as a full-time pursuit. In the millennial and especially gen Z generations, there are many with so-called "side hustles," some type of profit-making venture outside of their full-time job. Even without being involved in any kind of venture, millennials and gen Z exercise entrepreneurial spirit through the questions they often ask in their 9 to 5 jobs, in a continual drive to make the most of their self-perceived potential. What expectations of work have emerged because of our ability to be more entrepreneurial in our youth? How are those expectations perceived by those who are already in the workforce?

One Coin, Two Sides Model: Entitled or Entrepreneurial?

For this particular stereotype, the observable behavior is that millennials have different expectations for opportunities to contribute to and rewards to gain from the organization. From a traditional perspective, this can be perceived as entitled because modern talent has expectations of rewards and career growth that are different than before—when in the past, simply having a job with a regular paycheck was reason to be grateful. From a modern, top talent perspective, growing up has inherently involved entrepreneurial spirit and the idea of pursuing one's full potential, leading to workplace expectations that are most closely represented in start-up or entrepreneurial environments. In addition, modern talent is deeply aware that having a traditional job is only one of many options to gain a sufficient living in today's world. Table 3.1 summarizes the observable behavior, the two sides, and the supporting beliefs.

Exploring the Traditional Interpretation: Entitled

From a traditional perspective, entitlement sounds like this in the following scenarios:

> **Promotion-related:** "I've just started and I'm wondering when I will get a promotion" or "I've been here for six months and I think I'm ready for the next level."

Table 3.1   One Coin, Two Sides model for entitled vs. entrepreneurial interpretations of modern behavior.

One Coin: One Observable Behavior	
Different expectations for opportunities to contribute and rewards to gain.	
Side 1: Traditional Interpretation Entitled	**Side 2: Top Talent, Millennial-Based Modern Interpretation** Entrepreneurial spirit
Supporting Beliefs:	**Supporting Beliefs:**
❭ You should just be happy to have a job. A job is something that is given to you, and not everyone has the opportunity to have one. ❭ A job, at its bare minimum, is a way to earn a paycheck. I want my job to be fulfilling too, but first and foremost, I need to pay the bills. ❭ You should put in the time before asking for any rewards. You need to demonstrate that you are worthy before even asking. Why would the company give you something when you've done nothing yet? ❭ There is no difference today in the breadth of skills, knowledge, and experience of new hires or type of work we are tasked to do. Therefore, they still need to put in the time and "grunt work" before moving to strategic work. ❭ I feel threatened. Millennials ask for a lot of challenge and even if, by chance, they are ready for it, there's not enough room at the top for all of us. We can't all be senior-level employees. If there are too many people who have significant work responsibilities, I may be out of a job.	❭ I will take jobs with lower pay because I am after experiences that grow me and a life that is fulfilling. I'm not as interested in materialistic things as older generations, because it's been said since I was a kid that money doesn't make you happy. I believe in YOLO, and if I only live once, why would I want to work for you? I need a good reason. ❭ Jobs are only one way to earn income. Having a job is not having a special privilege. In fact, seeing how companies demonstrated in my formative years that they do not care about their employees, having a job is somewhat of a misfortune compared to other options today. ❭ I have been contributing my voice and skills since a young age through the Internet. I don't want to go backwards in my journey of self-development. When I can bring my full breadth of skills to work, I'm more engaged and willing to help the business grow their vision.

Source: Invati Consulting

❭ **Recruiting:** Attempting to negotiate better salary and benefits during the recruiting process.

❭ **Work plan:** Asking for more challenging work or showing poor performance when doing routine tasks.

❭ **Flexible hours:** Asking for flexible hours or simply not showing up when expected.

> **Skirting hierarchy:** "Hi, you're my VP right? I just wanted to introduce myself and maybe we could get lunch some time?"

> **The big picture:** "Why are we doing it this way?" or "How does this connect with the mission?" or "The strategy doesn't make sense to me." Wanting to provide input at a higher level or during a strategic conversation.

Consider Diane, an old high school classmate of mine. At age 15, she started showing up at university laboratories asking for a job. She had no experience. She had no education worthy of such a position; she wasn't even out of high school. Yet there she was asking. And asking for nine dollars an hour. Sound entitled? We will return to Diane's story to explore further.

The definition of entitlement is the belief that one is inherently deserving of privileges or special treatment. What was considered a privilege from a traditional perspective? Older individuals may believe that, at a young age, one should be happy just to have a job, and asking for more than that is asking for a privilege. For example, Dave, a boomer VP of regional sales, says, "In my day, we didn't know how much we were getting paid until we got the job and the first paycheck in the bank. We were told not to ask . . . by our mothers!" In the traditional workplace, things like salary, flexible hours, graduating from grunt work, and meetings with more important people were rewards. They were things you didn't ask for until you had proven value to the company. It was uncommon enough for a new person to challenge why things were done a certain way that it became a sign of a high-potential, future leader. From this vantage point, it's no surprise that when millennials ask, or worse, assume that these "rewards" are a part of the job, they are perceived as entitled.

In addition, recall that older generations grew up in a greater command and control, hierarchical world. The technology that controlled information at the time (radio, television, and print) was a very one-way interaction and had limited transparency. Older generations didn't know how much everyone around them was getting paid or what benefits they had. With less knowledge, there is less reason to ask such questions and hence previous generations were more accustomed (not necessarily happy about it!) to a small handful of people at the top, controlling destinies at the bottom.

What about workplace readiness after college? What messages about career choices were given to older generations when in school? Throughout the past 50 years, safety mindset, work experience, desegregation, and equality have changed enormously. Boomers and gen Xers spent much of their time after school free to roam around until dinner, with no concerns about safety. Life wasn't scheduled or monitored outside of school. Teenage jobs included babysitting, mowing lawns, and dog walking. College internships were often involved no more than making copies, answering phones, taking meeting notes, and bringing coffee. Observing others work was where the education happened.

In the 1960s, after the passing of the Civil Rights Act, the public education system started the process of desegregation, in which schools were no longer allowed to be built specifically for blacks or whites. This process continued into the 1970s, with challenges such as Hispanic/Latino desegregation and continued resistance from some Caucasian communities.[5] This struggle for equality extended into the workplace. If you were of another race or if you were a woman, career prospects were different. As a woman, you could have the exact same job as a man and be paid far less. There was a broader belief that careers were gender-specific. This clash is humorously brought to life in the popular 2000 movie *Meet The Parents*, where a young man in his twenties, played by Ben Stiller, is constantly teased and looked down upon by his girlfriend's father, played by Robert De Niro, for being a nurse. The traditional mindset was that men are doctors, women are nurses. In general, career options were relatively fewer for everyone in comparison to today. Common career paths included accounting, teaching, medicine, engineering, law, nursing, journalism, and agriculture, to name a few.

Education practices evolved as well. When in school, previous generations were exposed to different topics and teaching styles: a focus on textbook-based learning instead of active application or group projects; courses like Home Economics instead of Robotics and Programming;

and memorizing and listening to the "sage on the stage" instead of asking and contributing. As a result, in many workplaces, the traditional mindset meant that the ramp-up to strategic roles was a slow, arduous process that reflected the assumption that youth lack workplace skills and knowledge. Higher levels of work also involved having higher experience in diverse, team-based situations. Since many kids hadn't grown up traveling or in diverse, team-based environments, these were additional items to be learned on the job. Corporate career path models and individual goal setting processes reflect this outdated reality.

Another common assumption is that entitlement is caused by *all* millennials experiencing a much kinder parenting style and receiving awards as part of being the "trophy generation." I argue that there is much more to the story. As mentioned in chapter 1, the highly diverse millennial generation grew up under a variety of parenting styles. Yet many millennials, regardless of background, have greater expectations that are perceived as entitled. That implies there are other, more comprehensive reasons to explain millennial behavior. What do millennials and gen Z perceive as rewards and goals today, given the advances society has made?

Exploring the Modern Interpretation: Entrepreneurial Spirit and Maximizing Potential

Let's return to Diane's story, my high school classmate who strolled up to universities asking for a job with no credentials. What if I told you that today Diane is a graduate of Rice University and Harvard Medical School and is pursuing her residency in pediatric neurology? Still sure that she was entitled? When viewing her actions without context, as many of the individuals she approached may have done, she may appear entitled and wanting to be handed something for nothing. In retrospect, even in her own words, "It sounded utterly clueless. After all, many in the scientific community believe that 'talent' alone is the most important ingredient for a successful scientific career."[6]

What made her actions different from entitlement? It was the sheer perseverance of it all. She had been given advice that the way to get the job was to talk to the boss. She e-mailed 40 principal investigators, asking for a summer position. She also let them know that if they didn't reply, she'd be visiting their office in person and included a specific date and time. While many kindly replied with a polite decline, 10 people didn't respond. She dressed her best and visited the 10 people as promised. She received three offers. The first two were unpaid; the last offered her $8 and she asked for $9. She got the summer internship—and followed through with hard work!

We often judge actions instantly, without knowing the complete story. What may have sounded like another millennial being entitled was actually something quite different. As Diane has gotten older, she has realized that there is a distinction between being entitled and advocating for yourself. While many people may confuse the two, she's found that self-advocacy is just as important as innate talent. Self-advocacy is rooted in understanding and pursuing one's full potential, passion, and purpose.

And that is what's driving youth today—potential, passion, and purpose over a paycheck. Did you know that 72 percent of high school students want to start a business some day and 61 percent would rather be entrepreneurs instead of employees right when they graduate college?[7] Albeit, many high school students aren't aware of or deemphasize the hardships of entrepreneurship. Nonetheless, entrepreneurship is attractive because the desired rewards from work have changed for modern talent, from just collecting a paycheck to living life to the fullest. Because the idea of rewards and privilege has shifted, the questions and expectations of millennials have shifted as well. What I've found is that this shift is not about being entitled, it is about having an entrepreneurial spirit and passion for life fulfillment—and often, not being beholden to a sinking ship.

Growing up during the Great Recession, watching parents who spent their lives working for companies only to see their retirements disappear along with a reduction in benefits, has greatly disheartened millennials and distanced them from the traditional corporate track. Consider the example of the pension plan—an all but forgotten relic in today's world that honored employees' long service. Whereas many boomers may have woken up in their forties with a midlife crisis from lack of meaning in their life, millennials often feel having a quarter-life crisis is a better alternative. Having witnessed and heard since a young age that "money doesn't buy happiness," "you can do anything you want to do," and "follow your passion" with a wide variety of career paths available to them, millennials have taken the message to heart and are exploring a variety of ways to make this happen.

In the past, distrust in companies didn't stop people from taking jobs because there really wasn't a viable alternative. A newly formed belief is that *because of technology, millennials and especially gen Z have many more options outside of a traditional 9 to 5 to make a living.* Having a job is not seen as having a privilege in itself; remarkably, today it is seen as a disadvantage. In fact, those that make a living outside of "the system" are the ones who are idolized and respected by other millennials. What is so great about having a job that one should be grateful? We are all driven by the potential pains and pleasures we perceive. Boiling it down to a simple philosophy, with so many choices available to them, *I've found that millennials live their lives according to the idea of YOLO—you only live once—which describes the reasoning behind the fulfillment-oriented rewards they pursue. Conversely, they are driven by a pain, too, due to all the choices: FOMO, or fear of missing out.*

Organizations don't often realize that young people today consider traditional 9 to 5 companies to be just as risky as start-ups and entrepreneurial ventures. If you have to choose between working for a company where you will grow slowly and simply make a salary before they lay you off versus working for a start-up where you will learn a lot and it could go public or it could go bust, most younger people are inclined to choose the latter. Working for the paycheck? Why? They are only going to treat me like a number, reduce my benefits, and eventually lay me off. If I'm going to work 50+ hours a week, why not do it for a start-up or for my own venture where I can make a greater contribution, gain transferable skills fast, and potentially reap a greater reward? This avenue of thinking meets the need for YOLO and FOMO—emphasizing that a job by itself is not something to be grateful for that will make the most of life. In the long run, it leads to a new set of questions that *ask companies to prove the value for employees' time and effort.*

A second driver behind these questions is that the start-up and freelance mentality enables modern talent to use the skills they have been using their whole lives. Millennials have grown up with a significantly reduced barrier to starting businesses and having a voice. When once the adage was "children should be seen and not heard," today's world is couched in the anonymity and reach of the Internet. Consider how technology has created entrepreneurial spirit by allowing individuals to:

> ❭ Reach a target or extremely niche market

> ❭ Develop a following and be respected regardless of age

> ❭ Learn skills and gain knowledge rapidly

> ❭ Have ownership and create strategy

> ❭ Generate revenue with little to no start-up capital

Millennials and especially gen Z have more exposure to what it means to "be in charge" and be a part of a start-up atmosphere than previous generations, through experimenting with businesses at young ages. Contrary to outdated expectations, the new hire that just joined your company has probably done more than make copies and bring coffee during their internships, work experience, and course of study. While not familiar with every aspect of running a business, the new hire has probably been exposed to a customer-focused business mindset since grade school—a world of user experience, "likes," social media following, copy writing, managing image, communication, and influence. They've been exposed to incredible diversity and the global nature of the world, if not through traveling, then through the Internet. Joining a workplace means bringing those skills to work every day; they can't be turned off or compartmentalized to personal hours only. And why should they be?

Balancing YOLO and FOMO is about collecting experiences first, material goods later (or not at all). The rise in tiny homes, ride sharing through companies like Uber and Lyft, home sharing through companies like Airbnb and Couchsurfing, and even group living situations exemplify the emphasis on not spending significant money on owning material goods. Instead, millennials travel the world, go on adventures, purchase experiences at lowered costs through sites like Groupon. This mindset translates to the work world as well, with those questions around challenging work, strategic thinking, building relationships with leaders, flexible work arrangements, and so on. However, this pursuit and expectation for experience doesn't mean that millennials aren't putting work in. In fact, for top talent millennials, it means the opposite! They ask because they have experience they want to bring to the table now, not wasting an organization's time or their own when they could be making significant contributions.

Consider the story of Jonathan Barzel. In the five years since finishing his undergraduate degree, Jonathan has lived in four different cities in two countries and worked in three different industries. After graduating from the University of Memphis with his bachelor of science in mechanical engineering, he traveled to Sydney, Australia, where he lived and worked for the next two years as a sustainability consultant. He transitioned back to the US in the same industry, but pivoted for an opportunity to join a data analytics platform start-up in a business development role. Through this role and his philanthropic involvement in his city's start-up community, he took the exciting opportunity to join a Fortune 50 package and delivery company on their financial planning team. This group typically focuses on hiring post-MBA candidates who then help shape the strategy and direction of the company at the highest levels.

Jonathan did not act from an entitled "I deserve these experiences" standpoint at any time. He was driven by his entrepreneurial spirit, his desire to make the most of his potential and live a fulfilling life. Part of what enabled him to get global and start-up experience at such a young age was the infrastructure offered by digital technology, including the greater ease of relocation, the ability to find jobs, and the ability to grow his own knowledge about each situation. In his words, the common themes in all of these jobs have been threefold: a drive to have an impact—on those around him, on product and service quality, and on each business financially; a hunger for constant personal and professional growth and learning; and an emphasis on forming meaningful connections with his customers and colleagues. These themes define what YOLO means to Jonathan. Again, this was all in the five years since graduating—he certainly isn't missing out on life's experiences!

To summarize, this side of the coin is about breaking the paradigm that jobs are given and jobs are taken, that our work lives are somehow out of our control. While we all need to make a living to survive, millennials and especially gen Z are more willing to experiment with how to gain that living. They would rather fail at their own hands than fail to make money because a company took their job away. Same time and effort, different experience. In addition, top talent is coming to the table with increased business acumen and skill sets. They expect to change the obsession with age and tenure and instead focus on the skills brought to the table and tap into their potential from day one.

So when millennials ask for challenging work or to be promoted earlier, it's not about entitlement. It's about wanting to make the same kind of contributions millennials and gen Z are already used to making personally in a professional environment. When they ask questions about salary and benefits, that's because they perceive getting a job just as transactionally as companies view their employees.

■ ■ ■

Using the One Coin, Two Sides model, we now understand the changing ideas of reward and fulfillment that are occurring. This increased level of knowledge, experience, and expectations is not going away, because digital is not going away. While the traditional interpretation for gratitude is not right or wrong, the conditions of society today have brought forth a different attitude toward jobs. Modern talent, as a whole, will continue to assume the base transactional details will be present and for the real conversation to be about maximizing the win for both company and employee. Companies that transparently answer the "entitled" questions up front and then focus on capturing the entrepreneurial spirit of modern talent will be the ones to succeed and thrive.

Leveraging Entrepreneurial Spirit to Build Modern Organizations

Entrepreneurship is attractive to young people because of all the things they perceive they can get that they can't get from a company, especially the digitally enabled idea of bringing their full selves to everything they do and of living by the philosophy of YOLO. In the entrepreneurial environment, this looks like having the ability to:

> Work in a fun culture

> Be part of a fast-paced environment

> Wear multiple hats

> Have a lot of responsibility and autonomy fast

> Work on something that matters (to society and to themselves personally)

> Always see the big picture

> Be part of a goal-focused culture that is highly productive (in the modern terms we described in chapter 2)

> Always see the results of the work put in

> Potentially make a lot of money

From a traditional interpretation, where there were fewer options for careers, these were seen as privileges to have, and therefore a perception of young people being entitled has evolved. Instead, the key intervention is to move from naming the behavior as entitled to harnessing entrepreneurial spirit by cultivating an "intrapreneurial" culture.

First, we must understand what entrepreneurship means to young people. Older generations think about entrepreneurship as starting a "real" business—maybe a brick and mortar store or a venture that will require investment and one day could be bought by another company. Young people think of entrepreneurship as everything and anything that can support them financially. And, with the delay in marriage, often it's enough to support themselves. This could include freelancing, working from home at online jobs, e-commerce, or a combination of these. A study done by Millennial Branding and oDesk highlights that 90 percent of millennials believe that being an entrepreneur is about the mindset; only 10 percent believe it is about having actually started a company.[8] Most people aren't attracted to entrepreneurship because it's easy but because they want to escape the perceived pain of corporate culture.

Many millennials may never start a venture, full-time or on the side. There is a distinction I'd like to draw between entrepreneurship and entrepreneurial spirit. Not all millennials are entrepreneurs, but many have entrepreneurial spirit. Some essential components of entrepreneurial spirit are a deep commitment to doing something of significance, having a zest for life, and not being able to tell the difference between work and play. Entrepreneurial spirit is about pursuing your own passions and potential to the fullest. It is a highly motivated, purpose-driven state of being.

How can we transform corporate culture to leverage entrepreneurial spirit? Building an intrapreneurial culture encompasses both issues: it inherently addresses many of the growth-related questions that appear as entitlement and it harnesses the entrepreneurial spirit. The traditional concept of an intrapreneurial culture involves selecting a few employees who seem entrepreneurial to receive seed funding and try out an idea, as a reward. For example, a traditional approach is to keep an eye out for talent that questions fundamental approaches, takes initiative to suggest improvements, and in general acts like a future leader. Then, projects may be assigned outside of the daily tasks of the role. In this situation, the organization waits for ideas based on pure individual motivation and hopes managers notice. Another common approach is to hold an internal competition within a particular function, such as engineering or R&D, once a year to generate and collect the best ideas. Participation is generally unsupported, reliant on personal motivation, and an independent action. In contrast with these approaches, *to engage modern talent, shift from intrapreneurship as a reward and an individual activity to intrapreneurship as a part of every role and the community.*

In today's highly cognitive world, there is room for innovation, creativity, and learning in almost every role. This is something corporations need, even if they don't know it or want it. Some of the top qualities the C-suite say they are lacking in their leadership pipeline are things like agility, ability to deal with ambiguity, cross-functional team leadership, and innovative thinking. Many of these qualities are a part of an entrepreneur's DNA! In my research, the number one statement millennials find demotivating is "it's always been done this way." Instead, the first step to embrace entrepreneurial spirit and pursuit of fulfillment is to stop labeling it as entitlement.

One place where the rewards of this approach are evident is when millennials become managers and promote open idea sharing. Sherina Edwards is the youngest commissioner ever appointed at the Illinois Commerce Commission. Her management style is focused on an open group policy, where anyone can voice an idea and it is encouraged to think bigger than one's role. As an example, Edwards asked an executive assistant to think bigger than her role. The employee highlighted a gap—the commission had an awareness problem where the people of Illinois didn't know what the commission did. The employee suggested creating a one pager for customers. Edwards sent the created document to the whole organization, recognized the employee who conceived it, and ensured it was used. The employee said no one had ever done something like that, especially for someone in an administrative role. Edwards made sure to create an environment where everyone could exercise entrepreneurial spirit and received an idea that improved the brand awareness of the commission as a result. Especially in the public sector, those with a traditional mindset don't often see the value of this approach.

One of the simplest ways to build an intrapreneurial culture is to allow a portion of employee work plans to be free. The range of free time could be anywhere from 5 to 20 percent. Another possibility is providing a way to capture innovations. One way to do so is to ensure that managers stay in touch with free time spent and proactively collect feedback. This tactic is most useful when manager-employee relationships are strong. Sometimes, however, talent that is considering leaving may have a tenuous relationship with their manager, and having another way to appreciate their contributions can help reengage. Having an online social network or repository can be a great way to capture, discuss, and assess ideas. Often, the best ideas are overlooked, but it just takes one person to sponsor one.

Another important element of building intrapreneurship is to allow everyone to feel like an owner of the company. Every employee must feel like an owner of their role. In an intrapreneurial environment, the work plan is a discussion and open to input by the employee. Every employee also has a clear idea of the strategic vision of the company and how their role contributes. Even though they may not hold stock, like senior leaders do, if they know how their role impacts profits, they are more incentivized to contribute.

Anne Moder was one of the best managers I had, because she allowed me to feel like the owner of my role and my career. As I mentioned earlier, I made a career transition from engineering to training, but that move didn't happen overnight! Over three years, I had the opportunity to explore my career interests through one-on-one meetings with Anne where I constantly asked for more projects, more mentors, and planned out career moves way too early. (The folly of youth is thinking that you can plan 10 years ahead!) Anne could have approached our relationship with a feeling that I was being entitled asking for more, more, and even more, but she didn't. She approached me from the standpoint of being a sounding board, a collaborative partner, and we put projects on my work plan to reflect my needs for exploration. These projects included everything from engineering work to organizational culture work, such as leading the new hire network. They involved trying out new ideas as well. These experiences allowed me to gain significant clues about harnessing my purpose and potential. From a business standpoint, the support of my manager allowed me to focus on my projects instead of resenting them, stay engaged and remain at the company instead of looking for ways out, and exceed my role's goals instead of doing the bare minimum. Would it have been easier to discourage me than to collaborate and sort through the situations? I'm sure it would have, but I'm also sure there would have been a significant impact to my work.

In a successful intrapreneurial culture, employees don't feel as insecure about being promoted, gaining benefits, or gaining access to senior leaders, because they have the security that their ideas are valued, that they are allowed to have experiences outside their direct line of work, and that they can work effectively within the larger vision of the company. Consider answering many of these basic questions about salary, benefits, and career path up front during the recruiting process and while on-boarding. Then see what talent does with that information. Does the individual rise to the challenge, or do they prefer their existing role?

The importance of harnessing millennials' entrepreneurial spirit and leveraging their potential cannot be understated. With boomer retirements looming, millennials will need accelerated leadership development. In many cases today, the challenge has already been reversed—junior talent is managing senior talent. Thirty percent of millennials are already in management positions.[9] Dave, the VP of sales I mentioned earlier whose mother discouraged asking questions about salary, said it best when it comes to entitlement-perceived questions today: "If someone doesn't ask today I think there's a problem with that. That maybe they are insecure or desperate. So today, when someone doesn't have high expectations, I'm more worried."

Tales from the Trenches

There are many examples of traditional intrapreneurial programs, such as innovation labs, advisory boards, and internal subject matter expert communities. These programs, while certainly a great effort toward building an innovative culture, still fall short of capturing ideas across domestic or global scale and making innovation a part of daily work.

Consider the following two concepts of intrapreneurial culture in action as you build your intrapreneurial culture.

Case Study 3.1

Social Physics: Alex Pentland's Model for Idea Flow

The best modern intrapreneurial cultures focus on creating infrastructure, processes, and methods that enable idea flow. Lauded MIT professor Alex Pentland, one of the foremost authorities on data science and a serial entrepreneur, deciphered how ideas flow in today's digital world in his revolutionary book *Social Physics*. Pentland and his team at MIT have spent the last decade using the power of today's data science, commonly referred to as Big Data, to analyze social idea flow.

Regardless of what industry an organization belongs in, the elements he found that increase idea flow are extremely relevant to creating an intrapreneurial culture. Here are some ideas on organizational changes based on a small subset of his research:[10]

❖ **Create time to find and spread new ideas.** In day-to-day work, we often find ourselves overwhelmed with e-mails and meetings that can only be completed in a timely fashion by relying on ingrained, automatic responses. To fuel successful creativity and innovation, Pentland illuminates that we cycle between times when we are seeking out ideas and times when we are spreading a new idea among our networks to build consensus and then adopt the idea as behavior. Having validation of good ideas is just as important as generating ideas in the first place. Time in our schedules to find and spread ideas is a must to enable creative problem solving.

❖ **Provide connection to a diverse range of people.** A common millennial expectation is to have exposure across functions and levels, as well as to experts across the company through online social channels. Pentland supports the benefits of this approach by stating, "The most consistently creative and insightful people are explorers. They spend an enormous amount of time seeking out new people and different ideas, without necessarily trying very hard to find the 'best' people or 'best' ideas. Instead, they seek out people with different views and different ideas."

❖ **Having forums to turn information into ideas.** Just giving people data is not what makes them do something with it. Talking about it, online or off, is what makes someone create something new. As an example, Pentland shares a higher education case study: "People working in the same field, and sometimes even at the same university, had literally never met each other because the university administrators and the funding agencies thought it was sufficient to have the researchers read each other's papers and that they didn't need to travel to meetings or conferences. It was only when they began to meet and spend informal time together that new ideas began to bubble up and new ways of approaching problems began to spread."

❖ **Seek creation of safe spaces and positive team culture, where "failing" and experimentation is okay.** When it comes to intrapreneurial teams, psychological safety and group norms are more important than the actual members of the team. One of Pentland's most surprising findings is that the intelligence of a group is not determined by the intelligence, motivation, or cohesion of the individuals that make up the group. Instead, there are two primary factors that create an intelligent group where idea flow is maximized. The first is equal turn-taking in conversation. No one person dominates the conversation and all are equally contributing their voices in shorter lengths of time. Online discussion forums are one method that intuitively allows for equal turn-taking. Secondly, the social intelligence of the members allows for maximum creativity. Social intelligence refers to the ability to read others' behaviors and body language to make sure everyone is getting equal airtime and to see which ideas are being supported by the group. This is where older generations can help younger generations that may not be as used to reading body language.

These findings support the innate expectations of digitally enabled talent and go against the traditional approach to intrapreneurship. The idea of locating a few people who have shown entrepreneurial interest is not the way to harness innovation or engage the full potential of your workforce. Instead, making sure the collective whole has equal opportunities to interact, voice opinions, and build consensus is what sparks the most innovation. Online networks have a huge potential in helping to facilitate innovation. On the Internet, everyone enters as an equal. We can take turns, have brief conversations, and build consensus through upvoting ideas. Based on Pentland's extensive research, I believe embracing digital is a great way to spur intrapreneurship and engage employees of all generations.

Case Study 3.2

Intrapreneurship at Work: Cisco's "Innovate Everywhere" Culture

Cisco is a company of nearly 72,000 employees across more than 120 countries. Over a period of six months between 2015 and 2016, the Corporate Strategic Innovation Group rolled out an initiative called the Innovate Everywhere Challenge across the entire workforce and all functions to harness the entrepreneurial spirit of their employees.[11] In 2016, Cisco reported that nearly 50 percent of its workforce participated in the challenge, resulting in 2,000 teams and 1,100 ideas—supporting my research that there is an incredible entrepreneurial spirit waiting to be captured by employers. Cisco's work shows that, given the opportunity, a significant number of employees will opt in and voice their ideas. As a result, Cisco is making innovation an ongoing part of their culture through an initiative called My Innovation, which encourages all employees to submit their ideas year-round.

Alex Goryachev, the senior director of innovation strategy and programs at Cisco, shared what makes the company's culture work and how they created it. The goal was tough: to create a grassroots disruption from within, "to think and act like a lean start-up, while scaling up as an enterprise." Goryachev's definition of his efforts—an approach that "engages all employees, that transforms a large company into one that moves faster, that unleashes the next big thing"—aligns with the modern definition of intrapreneurship I introduced earlier. It's not about reserving entrepreneurship for the select few; it's about harnessing the collective power of grassroots movements.

The Innovate Everywhere Challenge was a six-month call to every employee at Cisco to innovate outside of their direct jobs, with gamification, guidance, clear goals, and judging criteria. Here are some of the key elements that made the challenge successful:

- ❖ **Grassroots power, from end to end.** The challenge began with grassroots momentum rather than corporate ownership by one silo. Existing disruptors, or "co-conspirators," across 16 of Cisco's functions were enrolled in designing the challenge.

- ❖ **Emphasized diversity and discomfort.** The challenge was open to everyone, regardless of tenure, level, or function. Current employee projects were ineligible. As Goryachev put it, "You are already getting paid to innovate as part of your regular job. We want you to think outside the box." They encouraged "ideators" to sell their idea and form cross-functional teams. There was also diversity in terms of bringing the outside in. More than 250 industry experts from both within and outside Cisco served as judges. Teams were encouraged to test their ideas externally and leverage external resources to grow their knowledge base and facilitate development.

- ❖ **Supportive collaboration platform.** The collaboration platform had a variety of strategically chosen elements to inspire, engage, and empower employees. It allowed for all ideas to be submitted, commented on, and peer rated. It allowed for people to recruit team members or seek teams with like-minded interests. The platform also provided guidance through each phase of development in a start-up. It was assumed that everyone was starting from ground zero and needed education on the fundamentals of entrepreneurship. Education-oriented "adventure kits" were built to enlighten employees on how to think and act like an entrepreneur. Employees also had access to mentors to help coach them through their challenge.

❖ **Follow-through.** The three winning teams were not only given seed funding to pursue their ideas, but three months off from their normal assignments and access to Cisco's Innovation Centers to pursue their groundbreaking innovations. They also received "corporate concierge services that helped remove roadblocks, expert technology resources, and mentors." The winning ideas were a venture to expand Cisco's offerings to include a suite of virtual/augmented reality collaboration tools, an intervention to use Cisco's existing collaboration tools to help people around the world with disabilities work remotely, and a new platform to enable deadline-driven digital media logistics.

Cisco's white paper on the challenge said it best: "In today's ultra-connected digital era, brilliant ideas can emerge from anywhere and anyone at any time, whether it's a seasoned executive or an early-in-career intern."[12] Besides the social and business impacts of the winning ideas themselves, Cisco has plans to move beyond this extraordinary success. They are considering other initiatives to capture entrepreneurial spirit such as a better algorithmic-based platform to match innovators to others to build teams as well as find mentors. They are also looking at ways for the community to contribute and engage through "virtual investing" in ideas.

The Innovate Everywhere Challenge is now one piece of Cisco's expanded My Innovation program.

Instead of staying focused on keeping things the way they've always been done, Cisco is seeking to use today's tools and ideas to capture the power of their global workforce in disruptive ways never before seen. Cisco is encouraging every employee to ask why, to be strategic, to be a business owner, because they see the benefit to the business, not only to create the next game changer for customers, but to make significant improvements to their everyday work processes.

Summary: From Entitled to Creating a
Thriving Intrapreneurship Culture

In this chapter, we learned how the expectations of the capabilities one brings to the workplace differ between a traditional and a modern perspective. Millennials have a tendency to ask questions and put forth expectations that sound entitled from a traditional perspective, when one was simply grateful to have a job and to slowly grow skills over a lifetime. In today's fast-paced, highly cognitive world where young people don't have to get a traditional job and bring a different skill set, millennials have evolved different expectations of workplaces that leverage their innate entrepreneurial spirit, tied to the philosophy of YOLO. Digital technology has decreased barriers to starting a business and provided more information about options for making income, enabling greater entrepreneurial spirit. From the stories of Diane and Dave, we heard evolving views of entitlement and rewards. While the traditional perspective served well previously, today's world has changed. To modernize the workplace, it's imperative to develop an intrapreneurial culture—*not just to attract and retain millennials and gen Z, but to develop all employees with the skills to remain profitable and thrive in a world where innovation is king.*

In addition to redefining being entitled as having entrepreneurial spirit, we learned that the definition of intrapreneurship is changing. Where intrapreneurial culture was once reserved for an elite few employees, efforts today should seek to improve idea flow across the complete scale of the company. Through sharing stories of Jonathan Barzel's five-year journey, Sherina Edwards' "any role can contribute" philosophy, and Anne Moder's guiding life-fulfillment management style, we heard some of the benefits of embracing an entrepreneurial versus an entitled mindset. From our research sharing, we saw how Alex Pentland's work highlighted that it is the diversity of ideas and broad discussion of ideas that make up the foundation of an intrapreneurial culture. The example of Cisco shows the success of efforts that contain these modern intrapreneurship elements that harness the power of our digital networks. In summary, we learned that the power of the collective is unleashed when people are given time to explore ideas and places to share and rate such ideas.

By embracing the idea that it's okay to ask questions and focus instead on the ideas that emerge, we engage, retain, and get high productivity from modern employees who seek to live a life of fulfillment and be entrepreneurial in their careers.

How Modern Is Your Culture?

How well do you think your organization is meeting modern talent needs? Read each statement and place an X in the appropriate column, then sum up your score. We have stated "my company" for the focus of each statement, but feel free to replace with "my immediate work group" or another community if it serves your purpose better. The assessment can also be found online at themillennialmyth.com/resources, where you can compare your answers with other readers.

	Strongly Disagree	Disagree	Neutral	Agree	Strongly Agree
My company has a variety of projects that challenge and excite our employees					
My company exposes our employees to people and projects outside my direct area.					
People understand how their work contributes to the company's overall goals.					
My company's career growth opportunities inspire our workforce.					
My company supports the concept of lifelong learning.					
My company fosters a sense of individual growth through assigned work, training, or other people.					
Everyone's ideas are heard, valued, and possibly implemented.					

More ▶

	Strongly Disagree	Disagree	Neutral	Agree	Strongly Agree
My company facilitates exposure to new ideas from our diverse internal workforce in some systematic way (could be an online platform, an e-mail newsletter system, etc.).					
My company facilitates exposure to new ideas from outside the company.					
My company moves at the right pace—not too fast, and not too slow.					
Total number of X's in each column:					

If the majority of your X's fall in the strongly disagree or disagree columns, your organization is leaning toward a traditional perspective that is at risk of disengaging modern talent. You may want to see where you can make some changes through reviewing portions of this chapter, trying the 10-Minute Champion ideas below, investigating our online resources, or reaching out to us for further help.

10-Minute Champion

What can you do to shift your organization toward a modern culture? Consider championing the following ideas in your work group, intended to take no more than 10 minutes each.

☐ **Facilitate idea generation.** Close your meetings with open-ended idea-generating questions: Is there anything we could do to improve our existing process? Is there anything you would change?

☐ **Facilitate cross-functional connections.** Pick one person on your team. Consider their work. Are there any connections or resources outside of your team (or company) that would be helpful for them?

☐ **Provide insight.** Bring one resource or insight that's external to your group (could be from another function or from outside your company) that you think would be interesting. Send it in an e-mail to your team, post it on an internal social network, or talk about it during a group meeting or an informal time such as lunch.

☐ **Step back and innovate.** Pick a part of your job that you do regularly. Take a few minutes to ask yourself why the task is done or why the task is done the way it is. Note any inconsistencies or improvements that could be made.

☐ **Create your own idea.** Feel free to create your own idea to build an intrapreneurship culture.

4

It's Not Hand-Holding, It's Agility

What we're experiencing is, in a metaphorical sense, a reversal of the early trajectory of civilization: we are evolving from being cultivators of personal knowledge to being hunters and gatherers in the electronic data forest.

—Nicholas Carr, *The Shallows*[1]

With the relatively recent introduction of digital technology in our lives, we all are experiencing its consequences for the first time. In the previous chapters, I have shown how digital technology has influenced millennial behavior and expectations around where and when we work, as well as the type of work we do and the skills we use. In addition, it has also greatly impacted how we process and use information. As was also established in the previous chapters, older generations form a different conclusion from observed digital behavior than millennials and generation Z.

Picture a millennial starting a job. Within the first week, they ask for feedback. "How am I doing?" they wonder. They want weekly meetings to make sure their performance is on track and to ask for support as needed. As a result, they achieve their metrics. A gen Xer, on the other hand, uses these meetings to understand the assignment and simply says, "I'll get it done." The gen Xer finds the necessary resources and achieves the metrics set at the beginning of the project.

A year later, it's performance review time. Which one is more likely to have high performance? Which is more likely to feel engaged? Which has the better relationship with their manager? It's not easy to tell which approach is right or wrong. Both approaches may work equally well, given the preferences of the individuals involved, because we all process and use information differently.

How has the experience of moving from cultivators of knowledge to "hunters and gatherers in the electronic data forest" impacted the older perspective? How has spending most of their lives in the same electronic data forest changed the younger generations?

One Coin, Two Sides Model: Hand-Holding or Agile?

For this particular stereotype, the observable behavior is that millennials desire feedback. From a traditional perspective, used to cultivating knowledge, this can be perceived as needing to be held by the hand. From a modern, top talent perspective, gaining information quickly and frequently is the way to be agile in today's hunter and gatherer world. Table 4.1 summarizes the observable behavior, the two sides, and the supporting beliefs.

Exploring the Traditional Interpretation: Needing to Be Hand-Held

When millennials ask for feedback and exhibit "needing to be hand-held" type behavior, it sounds like:

> Did I do a good job?

> Can you tell me how I'm doing?

> Can you help me make this better?

> Can you review this?

> How would you recommend I do this?

> Am I on track?

Table 4.1   One Coin, Two Sides model for needing to be hand-held vs. agile interpretations of modern behavior.

One Coin: One Observable Behavior	
Asking for feedback	
Side 1: Traditional Interpretation Require hand-holding	**Side 2: Top Talent, Millennial-Based Modern Interpretation** Desire agility
Supporting Beliefs:	**Supporting Beliefs:**
❯ The trophy generation wants praise for even the smallest things. I'm not going to give you an award just for showing up. ❯ I shouldn't have to give someone all the answers. It's okay to help out once in a while, but ongoing, they should have the initiative to find it themselves. Someone who has to be given the answer isn't a self-starter and probably doesn't have the right capability for the job. ❯ Cultivating deep knowledge and expertise takes time and is the best and/or only way to be successful. Some things you can only learn through experience. There isn't really a better way to learn it.	❯ Feedback is another form of learning and is not always related to performance. I can learn a lot and gain a lot more experience faster if I ask for feedback. It is the beginning of agile leadership. ❯ The more meaningful feedback I have, the more I can adapt to situations in real time. ❯ I am more likely to appreciate meaningful feedback than recognition for just showing up, which oftentimes feels inauthentic. ❯ There isn't value in working for the answer. Only make me work for the answer if there is value in me working for it. If the value is learning how to cut through red tape and bureaucracy, the feedback isn't for me, but for the organization: figure out more efficient ways to get your people the info they need to actually do their jobs.

Source: Invati Consulting

And it sounds like these statements . . . frequently. Like every other day. Given how much managers loathe the time and energy required for annual performance review processes, doing a quick performance review every other day seems absurd.

As mentioned in the previous chapter, when older generations were growing up, asking questions was not always encouraged by parents. Kids weren't recognized for every little thing they did. In fact, for generation X, it was quite the opposite. Gen X is often nicknamed the "latchkey generation," with many feeling unwanted when they were kids as the first generation to be impacted by high divorce rates. In contrast, affluent boomer parents wanted to give millennials what they didn't have when they were growing up. In many ways, millennials could be perceived as the most loved generation, through changes in the school system as well as parenting styles. Millennials are often referred to as the kids that got a trophy just for showing up. As such, because of this notion that millennials expect positive feedback at every milestone, previous generations often have a negative association when they're asked for feedback.

Another reason previous generations misconstrue the need for feedback is because of the exponential rise in information, in terms of both access and quantity. For previous generations, information flow was slower and one way. Individuals received drops from the proverbial leaky faucet of information. Today, we receive a fire hose of information that never stops. In addition to the quantity of information, there is a difference in the scope of information.

When a boomer or gen Xer started a job, it was possible to learn your way into the role, to spend time figuring things out without structured training or resources. Previous generations often believe that there isn't a need to get information quickly because when they first entered the workplace, they didn't need it as quickly and roles could be established into a long-term routine. They may also believe that employees should be able to sort through information on their own, because they were able to do that when they entered the workplace. Yet today, neither of these statements are true. The expectation for accelerated on-boarding and rapid adaptability has increased dramatically and has given rise to a term often used in the business world to describe the current environment: VUCA, or volatile, uncertain, complex, and ambiguous.

For example, I once had a manager tell me that to demonstrate proficiency in my role, it would take me eight years because there was no training to learn a very complex technology. I was dumbfounded. His expectation was that I would watch others, ask questions in a way that didn't bother people, and learn over the next three to five years. In his world, people spent 40 years working on the same manufacturing line, in the same organization. Nobody was going anywhere, and certainly not fast. Developing new people was dead last on the priority list. People weren't considered senior until they had put years of time in—someone who had been in his organization 15 years could still be considered junior. Moving forward, I didn't know if it was okay to ask for feedback, and my understanding was that there was no efficient way to grow either my knowledge or career.

He was living in the prime example of an old boys' network, common in the manufacturing world (and many other industries), where the boys that had stuck it out for years together were the ones with the power and knowledge. Information was kept close in the old boys' network and until you had proven you deserved access, you weren't privy to knowledge that would enable your job. You could work on a project for months, not know the strategic impacts, and have it cancelled because of your lack of knowledge and "in" with the network. This was the world he believed he lived in.

Yet the broader organization around him had changed drastically and he was cascading an outdated culture. Roles were designed to last three years, not five and certainly not eight. Projects changed in real time based on the ever-changing external environment. I watched others and asked questions, but I knew I would have been much more effective if I was given any kind of training—even a manual to read—rather than nothing at all. As top talent, I started creating my own manuals for the next person to use. There was no efficient way for me to be productive at my job. He may have thought that I was used to getting positive dings when messages came in, Likes on Facebook posts, and instantaneous gratification. While he may have perceived my actions as wanting to be "hand-held," I viewed him as a dinosaur—a survivor clinging to a bygone era.

In addition, reeling from the recession and battling demographic shift, most companies seek to hire experienced talent because they aren't investing enough resources in training and development. To meet higher than usual ramp-up expectations, millennials use their natural response of self-directed learning. Unfortunately, asking for feedback as part of the learning process is seen as negative behavior due to being a part of the alleged trophy generation or being accustomed to instantaneous feedback from digital.

Jackie, a talented young professional who transitioned from accounting to organizational development, experienced firsthand the challenges of meeting job expectations in a recession-driven corporate strategy. Over the past two years, Jackie has applied for over 500 jobs and, upon starting work, has been told less than three months later that she didn't meet the unwritten expectations in two cases. In each case, after a thorough and challenging interview process, she was hired to fill a role intended for someone with three to five years of experience. The unwritten expectations, however, were to ramp up much more quickly than possible. Despite asking for feedback so she could simply do her job, she was let go because the experience they were looking for was more in the 10 years' range.

The talent pool of experienced hires is low in her new field, and companies just don't want to take the time and investment to develop new talent. Jackie continually tried to meet unreasonable expectations by checking if she was on track through frequent feedback. In many cases the feedback was that she was doing great, which made it a complete surprise when she was let go. Today, she has finally landed a role that wasn't inaccurately defined in terms of expectations and provides support for her growth. She was successfully able to ramp up in the standard three to six months and has become an asset in her organization.

What other beliefs or societal norms do you feel contribute to the perception of needing to be hand-held? What is on the other side of the coin? Is asking for feedback a negative behavior? Does asking for feedback mean what traditional mindsets believe—that one is looking for a performance review or a pat on the back all the time? What is the intention behind asking for feedback from a modern mindset?

Exploring the Modern Interpretation: Agile

Is there a greater need for immediacy? Yes, yes, and yes! Neurological studies continue to demonstrate the impact of digital technology on attention span and social validation. However, the need for immediacy impacts everyone, regardless of generation. We are all more distracted by our devices and have higher expectations for immediate responses. I have been approached by countless parents who are frustrated by lack of immediate response to text messages. They often resort to e-mailing, calling, and texting for a response—within an hour! Perhaps, for some of the population more than others, getting awards and positive feedback for "showing up" also plays a part. But remember that with every change, even seemingly beneficial on the surface, new challenges arise. Kids who got trophies could also have had overloaded schedules, with back-to-back school and competitive activities. Overall, these components do not describe the full story, especially for top talent.

Modern top talent has another reason for needing feedback. Growing up, they saw changes happening very fast. As children, they moved from pagers to flip phones to smartphones all in the span of a decade. They moved from typing lessons to word processing software to complex software like coding or working in cloud-based applications. Because they were in the process of shaping their context for the first time, with each innovation they honed the art of rapid learning, of individual agility. They also witnessed the behavior of companies during the recession— where job security was constantly at risk and changes often occurred swiftly, without transparency. Although older generations experienced the same transitions, millennials learned different, digitally influenced ways to adapt to change.

What do I mean by agility? Not to be confused with the "Agile" movement or methodology, the agility I am talking about here is a leadership trait. In the *Forbes* article "Agility: The Ingredient That Will Define Next Generation Leadership," agility is discussed as "the ability to proficiently move, change and evolve the organization. They [agile leaders] 'seek pain to learn.'"[2] We often talk of agility from a larger organization sense: the ability to rapidly adapt to market and environmental changes in productive and cost-effective ways. But there is also the agility of a single person—their ability to adapt to ever-changing situations.

Modern talent believes that asking for feedback serves a single, critical purpose: it allows one to course-correct, to be agile in the moment. If you wait around for the answer, time is lost that could have otherwise been spent leveraging the answer. Asking for feedback is a way to get around the limited time and availability of training resources. It is a way to learn, learn fast, and grow your expertise. It is a way to reduce uncertainty around job security by knowing whether one is on or off track from expectations. For top talent, asking for feedback is *not* intended to be a full performance review or pat on the back. The feedback being sought ranges from what to do in a particular situation to assessing performance after a task is complete. This is a significant difference from the perspective of many managers, who struggle to disconnect feedback from performance management and instead associate it with learning. millennials want to show they are worthy of the job every single day, not just during annual performance reviews. They want to move as fast as the external environment around them.

In the case where one is tasked with finding the answer, the journey should be to serve a purpose. In the past, it may have been worthwhile to work through bureaucracy to find the right answer. Along the way, the employee may build relationships that will serve them throughout their career. However, today the expectation that a single, almighty expert will be there throughout one's career is wishful thinking. Rather, the roles are more consistent—who plays them may change and may change often. Relationship building is still critical, but it is taking a backseat to rapid learning.

Digital natives, who grew up in a world of global relationships, have become masters at assessing a broad variety of resources and filtering through to the right information—in essence, navigating a VUCA world. If there isn't enough formal training available to learn what I need, no problem! I can ask my peers, online or off, and crowdsource the best answer to meet my immediate need. If there aren't enough points of feedback for me to know if I'm doing well, I can ask my network to rate me. While millennials don't have every skill needed to lead in a VUCA world, asking for feedback is a foundational skill that plants the seeds for moving proficiently and changing in response to the environment.

■ ■ ■

Modern talent believes that they need frequent, meaningful feedback to course-correct and to focus on meeting goals more efficiently, while maintaining job security. Based on the One Coin, Two Sides model, we've found that the desire is to be agile instead of encumbered in today's information-overloaded world. From the traditional mindset, without the experience growing up in a world where skills needed change quickly, navigating change is not an intuitive ability. Yes, there are millennials who ask for feedback constantly because of anxiety when they don't get the instantaneous dings they are used to from digital tools. However, as a reminder, the behavior discussed here is based off of those who have successfully overcome the desire for meaningless information. If they hadn't been able to do so, they wouldn't have made it successfully to the workplace!

What some view as needing to be hand-held, from another lens it is viewed as the beginnings of being an agile leader. Both have elements of truth—our job is to mitigate the negatives and enhance the positives.

Leveraging Agility to Build Modern Organizations

How do we keep building on the innate ability to be agile? What other skills can we teach the youngest generation? How do we increase feedback and knowledge access for all, especially considering today's national and international workforce? To further Nicholas Carr's analogy that opened this chapter, in today's world, first we must find the right forest. Then, the right tree. Only then can we focus on the leaves and cultivate knowledge. Let's highlight three interventions to transform hand-held behavior to agility: an attitude shift, a new learning and development strategy, and ongoing feedback as a managerial tool.

The shift in attitude is to understand that every moment of feedback is simultaneously a moment of performance management and a moment of learning. Traditionally, we believe that feedback is related only to performance management because that is what the benefit is *from the company perspective.* But in today's world where modern talent expects to be an equal partner in the employee-company relationship, we must recognize that feedback is related to *learning* from the *employee's perspective*. Every moment of feedback is a moment of learning and as we ask for feedback, we increase the rate of learning, and we increase our individual agility.

To increase agility and productivity (as we discussed in chapter 2), organizations need to provide better access to resources and information. Internal systems today rarely reflect the personal systems outside of work. When searching for information, intranets are hardly optimized like Google or Bing. When looking for training or courseware, learning management systems have limited guidance on what to pursue in comparison to user-rated learning sites like Quora, Coursera, or even Yelp. Working within the limitations of today's poor internal technology, millennials seek to cast their net as wide as possible and ask for as much feedback as possible.

To leverage modern talent's need for agility, the greatest opportunity lies in expanding the training department's scope by moving learning outside of the classroom and by leveraging the strengths of the information technology department. By creating this crucial partnership, organizations can:

> Provide access to global relationships

> Crowdsource knowledge

> Create search algorithms that effectively filter through an organization's vast stores of knowledge

> Create infrastructure that enables learning such that knowledge transfer occurs

Learning and Development (L&D) departments today are struggling to figure out cloud-based, complex system challenges on their own. L&D would be better off leveraging the strengths of the IT department when it comes to evaluating software solution vendors, designing for user experience, creating systems that capture global scale, and understanding data analytics. By providing better access to learning both inside and outside the classroom, we address the aspect of agile millennial behavior related to asking for feedback on how to do something in the moment. In fact, the system to provide learning could be the same as the one discussed in chapter 3 that captures ideas and innovation!

Finally, to increase agility, a part of the manager's job should be to provide ongoing feedback—not just once a year at the annual performance review. In addition, managers should help create a culture where team members feel comfortable providing feedback to peers. Giving this level of feedback almost seems to be a necessity today, whether we want the feedback or not.

This is exemplified by my experience as a manager and being managed. Because I had less than five years of tenure, most managers at my company wanted to meet once per week to make sure I was on track. Older colleagues often mentioned that they felt that as you gain more tenure, the meetings become less frequent and it's a reward—the manager trusts you more to handle the work without the constant meetings. However, I felt a different need. Regardless of how much tenure I had, I would have wanted the meetings, not because I wanted to be micromanaged but because the feedback enabled greater autonomy with greater alignment between my manager's needs, my needs, and the business goals.

Interestingly enough, I saw the results of these different perspectives play out firsthand. By having my weekly meetings, I was able to adapt more often, have greater access to resources, and enjoy greater visibility with my manager and leadership. My performance was always highly rated in my yearly review and future-focused. Two of my gen X colleagues, on the other hand, only met with my manager once every month or even once a quarter. Their performance reviews were often based on resolving perceived performance issues.

When I became a manager, my direct report initially felt like it was a downgrade, reporting to a younger, lower-tenured individual than herself. However, she knew she would be working on the most innovative projects because of my work plan, so she was game to try out some new tactics and a new management style. She was also an employee who consistently had performance issues. I instituted weekly meetings, when she was used to meeting once a month. At first there was some resistance, but over time, a close relationship developed. I was able to identify learning needs for her much more rapidly and provide more meaningful coaching. She was able to give me feedback on my work and management style. During our time together, I was able to work with her to vastly improve on her performance issues, enable her to learn brand new software, and launch creative programs.

Unfortunately, after I left the company, she returned to her previous manager, with once a month (sometimes once a quarter) meetings. In our working relationship, feedback had created a necessary place of alignment and growth that enabled us to meet our business goals. It allowed us to filter through information and the changing circumstances. Without this feedback, essential understanding and productive relationships became absent, and eventually she was dismissed from the company.

I argue that a culture of ongoing feedback should be a separate discussion from performance management. One of the reasons why everyone wants to get rid of annual reviews and rankings is the sheer amount of time it takes for the manager. Simply providing more on-the-spot meaningful feedback has nothing to do with raises or ratings. Even if annual performance reviews are kept, having more feedback throughout the year will certainly improve overall performance versus if that same feedback wasn't given. You don't have to remove your annual performance review process to adapt to the modern world.

Through expanding access to learning and information opportunities as well as disconnecting the idea of feedback from performance appraisal, we can meet modern talent's need for agility in our information overloaded, highly cognitive world.

Tales from the Trenches

For organizations to leverage modern talent's innate desire for agility, we must reconsider what learning means and where it takes place. Let's explore two visions of learning in the future.

Case Study 4.1

Inside the Mind of a Digitally Enabled Learner

Scott Young, at 28, has spent the last 10 years pushing the limits of learning and productivity through a variety of experiments and research using today's tools. He has published over 1,000 blog posts with his research, which he started his senior year of high school. Young is a pioneer in the concept he calls "ultra-learning." One of his ultra-learning challenges was the MIT Challenge in which he used the OpenCourse-Ware (OCW) MIT initiative to assemble and learn the equivalent of a four-year computer science degree in 12 months. This was prior to the entrance of the many massive open online courses (MOOCs) like Coursera that are available today. Another one of his challenges was to spend "A Year Without English," where he traveled to Brazil, China, Korea, and Spain for three months each and learned the language through an immersive mindset. Young epitomizes a digitally enabled learner. Let's examine his motivations and recommended methods for learning.

The motivation for Young's ultra-learning work embodies many of the millennial behaviors we have already discussed. He is empowered by the ability to learn and work anywhere, anytime (not because he was too lazy to physically attend class!). For the MIT Challenge, he realized that he didn't have to follow the usual pace of the program—it was possible to work and take tests when he wanted, which encouraged him to take an accelerated approach of 12 months. He was also motivated by entrepreneurial spirit: doing more with less, experimentation, immersive experiences, and pursuing fulfillment. Despite not earning the actual degree, several HR representatives indicated that someone like Young is exactly who they would want at their company. That is, someone who could work on something for a year in depth without outside motivation. Young says, "It's interesting because it shows not just my skills, but some indication of my personality."

While Young is a firm believer that first and foremost the individual has to be motivated to learn, he shared the following ways organizations can deliver learning differently from his millennial perspective:

✤ **Promote insight-driven learning**. Instead of memorizing details and having a shallow understanding, Young promotes having a clear picture of how things work at a deeper level. As he puts it, "The best learners are people who sought a deeper understanding. Knowing why things are the way they were. They have a picture in their head, they are actively trying to fit the pieces together." For learning agility, consider this: If an employee is asking for feedback to improve their performance or get a recommendation, understanding why the feedback is what it is can greatly help to enable deeper learning for the long term. It may even decrease the number of feedback requests! If you simply tell someone "this is how I would do it" or "good job" but don't provide a compelling explanation, they won't understand the insight behind the recommendation or performance feedback.

✤ **Training on skills, soft or technical, requires new approaches.** Young says that trainers fall into the trap of rushing to give people all the details instead of laying out the context. As experts, we often feel that because there is so much ground to cover, we quickly gloss over why something is done. Young suggests flipping the approach: put more emphasis on the why, not just the what. Why is this learning concept or skill gap puzzling? Why is this concerning? Why is this a challenge? By answering these questions at the outset, Young says you make people curious instead of assuming that every point of feedback or learning is motivated by having to do it for work.

✤ **Emulate the environment that they are going to apply it to.** Another pitfall Young points out is that we often try to train using the easiest method possible for the trainer and assume the learner will be able to apply it easily in a different context. For example, if we train on a customer service skill through an e-learning platform, we assume that the learner will be able to apply the skill face–to-face, with a live person. Unfortunately, we are sacrificing a lot of accuracy in that situation. Pairing up with a colleague to practice, for example, would be a better method to increase learning.

❖ **Take advantage of MOOCs for ongoing professional development.**
Young believes strongly that we should all strive to stay on top of
our professional game and points to the power of MOOCs to meet
this need. MOOCs go beyond the e-learning typically offered by
companies by providing a profoundly global classroom community
and increased engagement through reflection-based assignments.
He encourages people to stay aware of courses in their field
offered on sites such as Coursera and posits that organizations are
underutilizing this tool for their workforce.

Young has found many other useful approaches to learning; these are
just a few that, from a millennial, digitally enabled perspective, make a difference. Using some of these methods, let's explore the simple example of
a safety training on using a fire extinguisher.

1. First, we could promote insight-driven learning by explaining why this
   training is important. Yes, it is important for safety and the technical
   skills to be gained. But it's also important behaviorally because you
   are learning a new instinctive reaction. That is why this training is
   puzzling, concerning, a challenge. This taps into the emotion of the
   learners and encourages a deeper context.

2. Second, consider emulating the environment. Obviously, the best
   training would be to have an actual small fire that one has to
   put out. But suppose you only have e-learning available. Would
   a multiple-choice test make sense to enable learning? Young
   proposes another approach: What if you physically or virtually had
   to aim something at a simulated fire? Now you're one step closer
   to the real situation because you are engaging the visual/physical
   parts of your brain and memory instead of only the visual/textual
   translation.

3. Third, what if there was a course available on a MOOC related to
   safety in the twenty-first century? (Surprisingly, one such course
   actually does exist from the University of Maryland titled "The Effect
   of Fires on People, Property, and the Environment.") Now, employees
   who use this option can learn from 10,000 other students around

the world through an engaging format about the real impact of fires, which, incidentally, the organization did not need to spend time or money to create!

Young takes a fresh approach to learning based on a digital mindset. However, today's best practices for instructional design often don't support making the most of digital mindset and modern learning needs. What would a modern learning design process look like?

Case Study 4.2

A Process for Designing Modern Learning Programs at Work

A 2016 report by degreed states that only 18 percent of employees would recommend their training department to other employees and 49 percent provide negative feedback.[3] It also found that the places where employees learn (say, outside the classroom, for example) are often where training departments have no presence. Because there is no structured presence, employees are often not getting the best information they could to leverage the scale and resources of the organization.

I partnered with Lisa M.D. Owens, owner of Training Design Strategies and a 30-year-plus veteran of the learning and development industry, for a year-long research project to create the Modern Learning Design Process, whose ideas and tools we have validated through workshops. How well do today's training departments meet modern learning needs? What do the best organizations do? What if the process to design learning kept the learner, instead of ease of delivery, firmly in mind? These are the questions we explored as we developed our process. Imagine if your training department used the following process:

1. **Understand the learner through building learner personas.** The modern learner is more diverse than ever, living in a world where change is the only constant and customizable learning options are an expectation. To design modern learning, the first step is to create

"learner personas" that allow us to understand the personality and behaviors behind our major groups of learners. For example:

* Do they work in a retail setting where there are new product and sales updates every week and occasionally deeper learning needs?

* Do they work behind a desk with a computer, or are they walking around with a mobile device?

* Can learning be delivered on the device used most often on the job?

* What instantaneous needs are most likely to come up—for example, a negotiation with a vendor, customer service response, or safety or troubleshooting need?

* What motivates the learner (competition, broad skill acquisition, etc.)?

We found that training departments are working off outdated assumptions of their learners. The departments that have reassessed their audience and understand the moments where the most learning happens are much more successful at providing modern learning environments.

2. **Modernize existing programs.** We highlight in our process that existing learning methods aren't going away, but they need to be modernized. We distilled modernness into nine key elements, including design choices like chunking, autonomous learning, and experiential learning. Old-school training could be revamped through adding modern design elements.

3. **Expand outside of formal learning programs.** We also need to expand our methods into where our learners learn today: not just in the classroom, but in social and immediate situations as well, a concept Lisa and I call developing Learning Clusters for Learning Touchpoints. Modern methods are focused on crowdsourcing learning—scary for L&D because they are used to controlling quality of all content. That makes sense for some training like compliance or technical skill training, but today there are many soft skill training needs in which there is no one right answer. The

best answer is going to be the one many people stand behind, not one single expert. Besides widening beyond formal training, L&D also needs to recognize that it is okay if not everyone takes every avenue of learning offered. The idea is to have a variety that will not be 100 percent utilized, but will be available for a diverse range of personas.

4. **Modernize your measures.** L&D's common measures of success are often related to number of people trained in the company and frequency of the training. Today, however, we need to measure L&D's ability to develop capability and improve employee performance. We found measures based on employee satisfaction with L&D services like Net Promoter Score or our own measure, Perceived Learning Value (PLV), are much more useful in rewarding L&D's transition to focusing on providing learning outside of formal opportunities.

Imagine if L&D departments were not just creators of content but facilitators of learning moments. Providing learning outside the classroom allows modern employees to get feedback on situations the instant they need it, whether that is through online searchable knowledge systems or through peer-to-peer connections. This approach also reduces dependency on nuanced manager relationships to provide feedback. Our process is more flexible, broader, while still containing the necessary elements for modern learning—it's inherently designed to be agile.

These case studies are both great examples of learning agility in the world of digitally enabled modern talent. It challenges what we used to hold important (grades over content) and how we could obtain it (slowly vs. rapidly). It challenges who needs to be in control of the content provided. Finally, it challenges us to provide access to these types of resources so we can meet the needs for feedback from our youngest information navigators today.

Summary: From Hand-Holding to Learning and Feedback Systems that Grow Agility

In previous chapters, we saw how digital technology has created new expectations in work hours, locations, and type. In this chapter, we explored the behavior of asking for feedback. We learned that the traditional perception of asking for feedback is based on a slower-paced environment and is tied to the process of performance management. When given too much feedback, the traditional interpretation may be to perceive it as micromanagement and reduced autonomy. In contrast, modern top talent focuses on feedback as an avenue for learning and growth, based on the need to quickly navigate an information-overloaded environment. It is the beginning of becoming an agile leader. Modern talent recognizes that the business need may be changing rapidly and therefore individual performance is more effective when it's able to course-correct throughout the year, rather than waiting for an annual performance review. This was exemplified through the story of Jackie and my own experiences being managed and as a manager. We discovered that this difference in perspective has its roots in the disruptive nature of digital technology, which has helped to create a VUCA environment and where effective work is governed by the ability to filter through vast amounts of information.

We also learned that improving learning and development infrastructure and providing more frequent feedback from managers are the keys to enabling employee agility. It's difficult for large organizations to be agile. Yet, through better L&D infrastructure and better manager accountability in providing feedback, a culture of individual agility can flourish. We need to return to a culture of "no question is a stupid question" and "no questions, no answers." Training departments need to own development outside of the classroom and partner with IT to catch up internal systems to today's standards. We explored different ways of thinking about learning and training design through the stories of Scott Young and the Modern Learning Design Process. In our time-crunched world of shifting demographics, we want all people to develop expertise quickly. Instead of seeing the need for feedback as needing to be hand-held, we should embrace the agility created by receiving ongoing feedback.

How Modern Is Your Culture?

How well do you think your organization is meeting modern talent needs? Read each statement and place an X in the appropriate column, then sum up your score. We have stated "my company" for the focus of each statement, but feel free to replace with "my immediate work group" or another community if it serves your purpose better. The assessment can also be found online at themillennialmyth.com/resources, where you can compare your answers with other readers.

	Strongly Disagree	Disagree	Neutral	Agree	Strongly Agree
The culture at my company makes it easy to give and receive feedback.					
I provide and receive feedback informally on work done at least a few times a month.					
My company culture encourages the idea of course-correcting as a reason for feedback, not just as a performance management tool.					
My coworkers and I are supported in pursuing learning and training opportunities.					
My company offers internal networking opportunities or systems that make it easy to learn from others.					
My company offers easily accessible resources to answer immediate questions and needs.					
My training department has a presence outside of the formal classroom (virtual or online).					
Total number of X's in each column:					

If the majority of your X's fall in the strongly disagree or disagree columns, your organization is leaning toward a traditional perspective that is at risk of disengaging modern talent. You may want to see where you can make some changes through reviewing portions of this chapter, trying the 10-Minute Champion ideas below, investigating our online resources, or reaching out to us for help.

10-Minute Champion

What can you do to shift your organization toward a modern culture? Consider championing the following ideas in your work group, intended to take no more than 10 minutes each.

- ☐ **Create a culture of feedback.** Give feedback to one person a day based on your interaction with them, or ask for feedback from one person a day. You could provide the feedback at the end of a meeting, via e-mail, or even via survey.

- ☐ **Identify your own course-correction needs.** Take a step back and review one of your high-priority, high-cognitive-load tasks. This could be a task you've been avoiding because it feels like a mountain! Spend a few minutes understanding why the task is feeling difficult. What blind spots or skill gaps do you have? What would help? Is there someone in your network you can bounce ideas off of or get feedback from? Is there a quick training or tool that would help you move forward?

- ☐ **Organize group resources.** One of the hardest things can be filtering through large quantities of information to find what you need. Consider a project you are working on. Would it help your group to have a guide to the resources (people, knowledge bases, other)? Consider creating an unformatted quick guide.

- ☐ **Create your own idea.** Feel free to create your own idea to building individual or organizational agility.

Add your idea and view others' ideas on the 10-Minute Champion at themillennialmyth.com/resources.

5

It's Not Disloyal, It's Seeking Purpose

Show me disloyalty and I'll show you detachment.

—Anonymous

One of the most notorious claims about millennials is their willingness to job-hop. For the last 10 years, we have been bombarded with statistics such as millennials will hold 10 jobs by the age of 32 and six careers throughout their lifetime. Looking at these statistics, it seems easy to conclude that millennials as a generation are disloyal to companies when previous generations were committed to spending a lifetime at the same job.

Yet, what is loyalty? Loyalty is typically defined as having a sense of duty, devotion, or strong support for an individual, cause, family, faith, or broader group. But loyalty is not given for nothing in return. Loyalty is based on a two-way relationship where there is an alignment of belief. Loyalty should not be confused with servitude.

Despite the perception of millennials as job-hoppers, many people can identify with them regardless of generation. They recognize that the Great Recession has created a job climate that doesn't enable retention. Also, many people started out their careers believing it would be a linear path, but found that their path had many twists and turns along the way. I've met several such individuals: a person who, in a 30-year-long career, started in pattern making, went to chiropractic school, and finally ended in a sales career; a long-time lawyer who became an entrepreneur running a canned food cooking store; an interior designer who became a director of education; and many more. There are many who believe job-hopping is the best way to grow salary and career. There also many who were able to spend 30 years at the same company.

If disloyalty causes detachment, inspiration and connection cause loyalty. As we will see in this chapter, the road to loyalty is to give people cause to be loyal, to give them something to believe in. Furthermore, we will see that disloyalty is not a millennial phenomenon but a symptom of corporate instability and is something all generations can agree on.

One Coin, Two Sides Model: Disloyal or Seeking Purpose?

For this particular stereotype, the observable behavior is that millennials leave companies within three years, if not less. From a traditional perspective, this can be perceived as disloyal. From a modern, top talent perspective, this is a side effect of the global recession and is a call to action for corporations to be held to higher standards and earn back employee loyalty that they are no longer entitled to. These higher standards involve cultivating a strong foundation in values and mission that highlights the impact the company is making on the world, and how each employee contributes to that impact. Table 5.1 summarizes the observable behavior, the two sides, and the supporting beliefs.

Exploring the Traditional Interpretation: Disloyal

From the traditional perspective, people often believe that millennials are primed for immediacy and when they don't get what they want, they leave. However, just like in the other chapters, there is more to the story.

Most people in previous generations, especially when working for large corporations, expected to work at a single company for 30 to 40 years (and expectations were relatively fulfilled in comparison to today).

Table 5.1   One Coin, Two Sides model for disloyalty vs. seeking purpose interpretations of modern behavior.

One Coin: One Observable Behavior	
Questioning or challenging people equally, regardless of tenure or level.	
Side 1: Traditional Interpretation Finding a new job on average of every three years.	**Side 2: Top Talent, Millennial-Based Modern Interpretation** Seeking purpose; compelled to have an impact
Supporting Beliefs:	**Supporting Beliefs:**
› It's riskier to leave an unstable company than to stay around and get a paycheck as long as possible. › It should be possible to stay at a company for 30 years. Reality has changed and that is scary! But I still sometimes act as though continued employment is fairly certain. › I'd like to make a difference through my work. But I've been around long enough to know that some companies facilitate giving back and some don't. If I really want to give back, I can always volunteer or do something meaningful outside of work. › This new generation is primed for immediacy. If they aren't immediately given a promotion or a raise, they want to leave. They don't understand that it takes time to develop your career. › The company needs to come first, the individual second. Don't make your success more important than the team's.	› Companies aren't entitled to my loyalty after everything they have done to employees who stayed with them 30–40 years in the past. I have to be careful about what company I choose to stay at for a long time—and even then, I can't expect that there won't be layoffs. › I want to work for a company that proves it cares about its employees, the surrounding community, and the world at large. I have to look out for me and what's best for me is to gain as many transferable skills as possible, and make as big of an impact as possible while the company is still interested in keeping me. › We are facing huge, global problems today. I have seen individuals as well as organizations have a huge impact on addressing them. I want to be a part of something long term that is making a difference.

Source: Invati Consulting

If one so desired, it was possible and probable to stay at a company long term. Regardless of generation, most people tend to agree that this is no longer the case. In my research, one thing generations can agree on is that companies, being profit-focused, have lost their way when it comes to earning the loyalty employees gave them in the past. According to the 2014 *Workforce 2020* report, published by SuccessFactors, one of the top three concerns of employees globally is that their position will change or become obsolete. In the US, one out of every four employees share this concern.[1]

Yet older generations often still can't understand why a millennial wouldn't wait until the actual day comes when they lose their job. Older generations experienced a time of greater job security and have a greater tendency to assume the job will be there (or at least, not to leave before they let you go!). As mentioned in chapter 3, millennials are well aware that there is more than one option for earning an income today. Modern talent doesn't share the belief that working for a paycheck is a good enough reason to stay at a company.

Another reason relates to life stage and responsibilities. Older generations are reaching life stages and situations, such as supporting and funding education for a growing family (gen X and young boomers) and reestablishing retirement funds post-recession (late boomers), that make leaving a job high risk. These situations promote staying with the job, no matter how bad, as long as possible. In contrast, millennials globally have delayed marriage and don't necessarily feel the pressure to work just for the paycheck. They are at the beginning of their lifelong career journey. They are looking for ways to reduce their dependency on corporate jobs to provide for them. It is actually seen as a greater risk to stay with a company that isn't doing well—you may risk becoming obsolete yourself from a skill perspective or miss out on growing a foundation for the next job.

Many generational studies highlight the value of compartmentalizing work from other parts of life for older generations. If they can't pursue value-based work at their job, they can pursue it outside of work. For example, my mother is an accountant and has spent spare time volunteering to help low-income individuals complete their tax returns. From a traditional mindset, a corporation's first job is to produce profits and a distant second (or third or fourth . . .) is to contribute back to society. What other beliefs and societal norms do you think influenced the perception that millennials are disloyal?

Exploring the Modern Interpretation: Seeking Purpose

What creates loyalty for modern talent if not the paycheck? Recall, based on its definition, that loyalty is created by providing something to believe in. Specifically, modern talent is inspired and attracted by doing social good.

After witnessing the impact of the Great Recession and corporate irresponsibility on their parents (facilitated globally by digital transparency and more open parenting styles), millennials have developed high selectivity when it comes to staying at a company long term. As we have discussed, it is 100 percent seen as a choice and a two-way street, where the companies must earn loyalty of employees. Millennials know that there are compensation and benefits associated with working a full-time job. However, forgoing a traditional job seems less risky since they also know about the many people who have worked from home, pieced together a freelance career, or earned income online successfully.

Millennials have gained insight into global challenges from a young age and appreciate an increased capability to make a difference through grassroots initiatives because of the advent of digital technology. Consider the opportunities to contribute to causes through sites like Kiva and Facebook. We are also well aware that global challenges such as climate change will only be solved if large organizations, governments, and universities collaborate together. According to a 2014 report on millennials and social responsibility by Deloitte, more than 80 percent of millennials believe businesses can help solve the biggest challenges they see today, including income inequality, climate change, and resource scarcity.[2] According to Millennial Impact, an organization devoted to studying millennials and their relationship to social good, corporate social responsibility and related initiatives are the third biggest factor when making the decision to accept a job.[3] When the company's cause-related work is talked about during the interview process, 55 percent of millennials were influenced by the knowledge when accepting a job.[4] Top talent often has a strong belief in working for organizations that mirror their own sense of purpose and desire for social good. These organizations appear to be few and far between.

Modern talent believes that a company that cares about the surrounding community is more likely to care about their employees. Therefore, a reason to believe in and inspire loyalty emerges. Does holding organizations to higher standards of social good hinder or help profits? What do effective corporate social responsibility programs look like from a modern lens?

Leveraging Millennial Values to Build a Modern Organization

One of the key ways organizations are focused on "solving the revolving door," especially regarding millennials, is by assuming they can't retain employees and instead leveraging them while they are there. One of the talent development executives I spoke to mentioned that they are revising their career-path model to allow for assignments that are one or two years in length instead of their standard three to five. Ironically, I've found this may reduce engagement and actually increase turnover because it reinforces the perception that the company doesn't have room for the employee longer term. The only way to solve this is to strive to become a company that people want to work for. In addition to the interventions discussed in previous chapters, another key intervention is to build a modern corporate social responsibility culture, *one that is more than financial contributions and fund-raisers*. It's about creating corporate social responsibility that resonates with modern talent (and consumers) based on our One Coin, Two Sides model.

Similar to Abraham Maslow's hierarchy of needs for individuals, I propose that there is a perceived hierarchy of needs for businesses to fulfill. In the first stage, we expect businesses to have a viable idea and make profit on a small scale. The goal is survival, analogous to a person's physiological and security needs. In the next stage, businesses need to scale up and make profit on a large scale, becoming a part of the fabric of society as an essential product or service. This is analogous to the individual stage of love and belonging. The next stage, then, is to start moving beyond profit and into social impact and mission. Similarly, in an individual, the last stages are esteem and self-actualization. The expectation is that companies that have been around for a long time or are extremely successful should be able to maintain the status quo while expanding more influence and contribution to social good.

Especially for today's big Fortune 500 businesses, Wall Street pressures of high growth may be enabled by investing in social responsibility initiatives. As corporations meet their base needs of profit, both talent and consumers expect them to evolve to meet metrics of social good. Social responsibility increases brand awareness, attracts talent, decreases turnover, and ultimately sustains the communities that businesses reside in. Imagine the ghost towns of the mining industry or the towns that aren't listed on the top 10 places millennials want to live. We can see what happens when a business stops investing in their surrounding community. Many corporations today tend to simply move to another community that someone else has invested in, but this certainly comes at a cost.

Loyalty is earned when companies show that they truly care: care about their employees, care about society, and care about the environment. Knowing that highly established companies are empowered to make positive impacts, but often choose not to, inspires disloyalty. Instead, working for a company that focuses on meaningful impact, from the executive level down to the frontline employee, is the new expectation. If you want millennials (and just about anyone else, really!) to be motivated and loyal, organizations need to value positive impact in two ways—at the organizational level and in the day-to-day work of the employee. On an organizational level, having a strong social responsibility mission is imperative to millennials. Good social responsibility programs have three key characteristics:

1. Customizable employee involvement

2. Genuine authenticity to do good

3. Are not limited to financial contributions

From an individual level, having a work plan that clearly ties to the business mission and vision is important. Work plans should be meaningful and every employee should be able to articulate how their role contributes to the business. If the mission and vision have been articulated clearly to encompass the business's benefit to society, employees inherently will understand the connection of their work to social good.

Tales from the Trenches

Let's explore several case studies of organizations that galvanize support and loyalty through social good.

Case Study 5.1

Turning Around Turnover Through a Cultural Movement

The retail industry has one of the largest turnover challenges of any industry. Yet TCC, one of the largest Verizon Premium retailers, has a turnover rate of 45 percent—significantly less than the industry average of 66 to 80 percent for part-time employees. Although not by design, TCC attributes their decreased turnover to their program "The Culture of Good," initially spearheaded by Ryan McCarty and today a cultural movement across the workforce. In addition to decreased turnover, TCC has enjoyed increased engagement. Ninety percent of employees between the ages of 25 and 35 report that the Culture of Good gives them a sense of fulfillment at work. The movement was started when Scott Moorehead, CEO of TCC, created a single role for corporate social responsibility and hired full-time pastor Ryan McCarty to lead it.

The Culture of Good is based on a philosophy of using moments to build a movement. Here are some of the moments the program championed and the elements that made them successful:

❖ **Easily scalable.** When designed by one man with no staff, an initiative must be simple and easily scalable. McCarty's prior nonprofit experience taught him to start small, scale big, and create a cadence of moments to build a movement. When the program launched in 2013, McCarty started by distributing 60,000 backpacks filled with school supplies to 1,600 employees in 28 states. To build a movement, McCarty went on to build a cadence of similar moments in which, today, 91 percent of stores are involved. Every quarter, TCC has an event, with themes like Teachers Rock Supply Giveaway, Heal the World, Stop Hunger, and the original Backpack Giveaway.

✤ **Authentic intention.** The Culture of Good wasn't designed to improve profit, decrease turnover, or increase engagement; its purpose was just to do good. It is based on authentic giving that every employee and the community can participate in. TCC is in the service industry, not just retail, with stores located in local communities across 42 states. TCC sees serving those communities as an integral part of serving their customers and employees and, therefore, is related to their core business and profits. The unintentional increased brand awareness worked: 68 percent of their employees report that their store has gained new customers because of the Culture of Good.

✤ **Employee choice and autonomy.** To keep the events scalable, some things are held consistent across stores: theme, calendar date, and budget. But every store has flexibility in determining the details of the localized parties for the events. Employees are given 16 hours paid time off every year to volunteer, whether that volunteer time is during or off work hours. Employees are also free to contribute ideas to grow the effort like adding recycling, which was suggested by new hires. Stores can also choose local charities that they would like to raise donations for, which TCC matches throughout the year.

✤ **Essential to employee development and therefore, company culture.** Over time, McCarty ensured that the Culture of Good went beyond the events into becoming a sustainable part of the company culture by making it an essential part of each employee's role. Based off a year-long pilot group of "ambassadors," today, performance evaluations for each employee are based 50 percent on direct job performance and 50 percent on culture. As a result of their participation, employees grow their internal network, have greater visibility from a career perspective, and learn valuable transferable skills.

By engaging McCarty to create an authentic cultural movement, CEO Moorehead freed his company from solely focusing on numbers to harnessing the power of intangibles—and found amazing results. The success has been so positive that McCarty has enrolled other companies in the effort. The backpacks this year number 135,000 and another company has been so inspired by TCC's work, they are partnering to give an additional 100,000 backpacks. As a result of interest from other companies, TCC has packaged what they have done to help other companies build movements of their own that connect with their employees, customers, and community. The Culture of Good is now an operating system that helps companies discover or rediscover their cause.

The example of TCC highlights how small changes, such as creating a single role and empowering employees, can result in large movements. TCC's approach was to leverage the grassroots desire to do good to create a culture that spreads to every employee, beyond financial contribution. Lower turnover, increased engagement, identification of high-potential talent, and increased customer acquisition are only a few of the benefits to TCC. The company has earned the loyalty of the employees, the customers, and the community at large through their work.

Case Study 5.2

NEWaukee—Millennials Influencing Corporations to Invest in Community: A Grassroots Approach to Inspiring Two-Way Loyalty

Angela Damiani is the 30-year-old cofounder of NEWaukee, a social architecture firm and one of the most unique organizations I've found: it turns the idea of corporate loyalty on its head. Damiani, choosing to move to Wisconsin as a young adult, saw many of her peers leaving the state for more modern, urban centers. She saw corporations leave as well, unwilling to invest in creating a thriving community. Damiani sought to change the paradigm and picked up the reins corporations in the area had left behind. Damiani, her business partner Jeremy Fojut, and the rest of the NEWaukee team have created a diverse range of events, education, and community by enrolling millennials and local businesses to participate. Ultimately, these events help to attract and retain talent in Wisconsin. Each event or project is unique based on the community's needs and existing infrastructure. Here's a snapshot of some of NEWaukee's initiatives:

❖ **West Wisconsin Avenue revitalization.** In the launch city, Milwaukee, like many cities, there was an abandoned retail corridor with shuttered buildings, but cheap rent. NEWaukee's team realized that many city residents had misperceptions about safety and so they created an event called the Night Market to revitalize the area. Local businesses were dubious, but NEWaukee was able to get 100 artists to create an open-air, free marketplace–style event with 40,000 in attendance the first year. Last year, vendors sold over half a million dollars' worth of goods. As a direct result of this event, the area is becoming revitalized, exemplified by the repurposing of an old urban mall nearby. The event helped attract a new owner for the property and they are reapplying lessons learned from the Night Market to develop an urban market, with input from NEWaukee on the design.

❖ **Penrod.** As a new start-up company to the Wisconsin area, Penrod was interested in recruiting talent. NEWaukee helped them sponsor nighttime music events where Penrod's existing 10 employees could become a part of the community. By sponsoring regular events, they now have 50 employees and recently won an award for the best place in Wisconsin for young professionals to work. This is one of the clearest examples of a company investing in the community and getting a return, or return on community (ROC) as NEWaukee calls it.

❖ **YPWeek.** The original event that started it all at NEWaukee is an annual event for young professionals to connect with corporate and nonprofit leaders, network with each other, and experience their community. The inaugural event took place in Milwaukee and has expanded to 150 events in 15 cities across Wisconsin with an astounding attendance of 12,000 young professionals. The week showcases events that highlight unique parts of the community, organically creating reasons for people to stay as well as providing a lot of opportunity for friendship making.

Damiani's message to corporate is this: "The world is un-siloed today. Why do we pretend that the corporation and the community and the government are all silos? We can all win by investing in our local communities. You can find more talent locally; the talent will stay in the community because they like it; and spend their dollars growing company profits and the economy. Our hope is to help people look critically at the place they live, to see its potential, and to shape it as a place that everyone wants to be a part of." NEWaukee, although consisting of over 200,000 subscribers, still lacks significant corporate investment. Damiani finds that corporations tend to see investing in community as a part of external relations instead of as core to their profitability. Corporations in Wisconsin, if they choose, could use the existing infrastructure NEWaukee has built and shortcut their path to gaining employee loyalty.

Overall, NEWaukee is a powerful model of how to increase employee engagement and retention by investing in creating thriving communities, whether that investment is made by companies, government, or the people themselves.

Case Study 5.3

Corporate Social Responsibility in a Global Company

Yum! Brands operates 43,000 restaurants in 130 countries, including such familiar names as Taco Bell, KFC, and Pizza Hut.[5] Yum! is another fantastic example of a company that has been able to create better internal culture and increased profits while nurturing a strong culture of social good. In 2015, Yum! reported over 40,000 hours volunteered by employees and franchises.[6] There are many examples of social good initiatives, spanning four categories: food, community, people, and environment. Let's walk through one of their many examples, the specially abled restaurants initiative.

In 2008, a Yum! team in India proposed a new social project whose goals was to have at least one KFC location in every major Indian city run 100 percent by teams that are hearing and speech impaired. It became a part of their work plan to bring this vision to life.[7] David Novak, soon-to-be retiring chairman, commented in an *AMA Quarterly* magazine article, "During a visit to one such store in Bangalore, I was amazed to see how the kitchen works with lights replacing buzzers and bells to tell staff when food is ready. At the counter, there are menus customers can point to in order to communicate orders. There are even table tents to teach people basic sign language, which the customers love."[8] By 2015, the effort expanded to 21 stores across the country, employing over 300 team members, seven shift managers, and one assistant restaurant manager, who are all speech or hearing impaired. The initiative also spread to other countries with Yum! presence, including Thailand, Pakistan, Egypt, and Spain.[9]

The Yum! example highlights how a company of 1.5 million employees in a competitive industry can grow market share, brand recognition, and engagement through social responsibility. It also continues to reinforce the same elements that work: giving employees autonomy to contribute ideas, allowing work plan time to be devoted to doing good, authentically helping the community, and focusing on more than just financial giving.

These examples span a variety of industries and paint a picture of the loyalty created through pursuing social good as a corporate value. Whether you are in the retail sector with consistently high turnover or fast food or a local community, there are a wide variety of initiatives to consider.

Summary: From Disloyalty to Recapturing Organizational Purpose

In this chapter, through the One Coin, Two Sides model, we learned that millennials' relationship to a company has changed because companies themselves have changed. While we would like to be able to rely on companies as in past times, people from all generations agree that this is an unrealistic expectation. Employees in general feel that companies are no longer entitled to loyalty, and those that show they care about social good earn back loyalty more successfully than those that don't. In previous chapters, we explored how the emergence of digital technology has influenced new expectations for how, when, and what we work on, as well as what enables our most effective work. In this chapter, we furthered this discussion by exploring how digital technology provides further transparency into corporate actions and global events, as well as the tools to effect social good.

In order for organizations to create loyalty, we introduced the concept of a hierarchy of needs for businesses where once a business has reached a point of sustained survival and brand recognition, the next step is to pursue a strategy of giving back. We then discussed two ways in which an organization can create effective social responsibility. One is to nurture a corporate social responsibility culture, which includes a mission that discusses the impact of the business on society and ways for employees to contribute beyond financial means to the initiative. The second is to have work plans that clearly connect to the business mission.

Employees are trying to hold corporations to higher standards. While the traditional belief is that investments in social good require money and time away from work, the case studies we explored show how much can be done with little. In the example of TCC, one man created a movement in which new customers have been gained and brand recognition has improved. The example of NEWaukee shows how investing in creating thriving communities retains and engages talent. Finally, the example of Yum! Brands shows how the same elements can be used in a global company. These case studies represent only a small estimation of the success that can be gained for companies, employees, and communities by investing in social good.

How Modern Is Your Culture?

How well do you think your organization is meeting modern talent needs? Read each statement and place an X in the appropriate column, then sum up your score. We have stated "my company" for the focus of each statement, but feel free to replace with "my immediate work group" or another community if it serves your purpose better. The assessment can also be found online at themillennialmyth.com/resources, where you can compare your answers with other readers.

	Strongly Disagree	Disagree	Neutral	Agree	Strongly Agree
My company cares about earning the loyalty of its employees.					
My company cares about its impact on the world.					
My company cares about sustainability.					
The mission or purpose of my company makes me feel my job is important.					
My company contributes more than financial investment to social good.					
If they choose, employees can participate in efforts for social good at my company.					
Total number of X's in each column:					

If the majority of your X's fall in the strongly disagree or disagree columns, your organization is leaning toward a traditional perspective that is at risk of disengaging modern talent. You may want to see where you can make some changes through reviewing portions of this chapter, trying the 10-Minute Champion ideas below, investigating our online resources, or reaching out to us for further help.

10-Minute Champion

What can you do to shift your organization toward a modern culture? Consider championing the following ideas in your work group, intended to take no more than 10 minutes each.

- ☐ **Inspire yourself.** Consider one way in which the work your company does benefits society. Spend a moment considering how your work ties into the company's goals. Make a note of it and use it as a reminder if you need to feel inspired in the future.

- ☐ **Inspire others.** Consider other ways you can highlight how your company has a positive impact, such as changing your e-mail signature to your company's mission or values statement or providing detail in your LinkedIn profile. Share your thoughts at the next group meeting or on your internal social network.

- ☐ **Learn your colleague's community ties.** Ask a colleague, "What is one way our local community impacts you in a positive way?" The answer could uncover a colleague's formal cause work, participation in a local organization, or something as simple as going to a weekly farmer's market and supporting local businesses. You may learn something that could be a great place to sponsor events, like TCC's work in local communities. Or simply, you may have demonstrated that you value getting to know a colleague better.

- ☐ **Create your own idea.** Feel free to create your own idea to building loyalty through demonstrating an authentic desire for helping social good and community.

Add your idea and view others' ideas on the 10-Minute Champion at themillennialmyth.com/resources.

CHAPTER

6

It's Not Authority Issues, It's Respect Redefined

I do not want my house to be walled in on all sides and my windows to be stifled. I want all the cultures of all lands to be blown about my house as freely as possible.

—Mahatma Gandhi

To rise to a leadership position is a difficult, time-consuming venture. It is a coveted position of respect, influence, and prestige that relatively few hold. A similar journey, although more inevitable, exists when holding a tenured position or building expertise in a field. Becoming a leader or tenured individual transforms a person in both positive and negative ways. For example, we admirably gain the ability to manage situations of increasing complexity and scale. But for many, these positions can also create a false sense of security in our expertise and position. We become confident in what we have always known, what has gotten us here. We let our house become stifled, navigating unexpected situations without considering what's happening outside in the present moment. As is commonly said, "What got you here won't get you there." Instead, a high-performing leader or tenured individual is someone who demonstrates a balance between their honed expertise and their ability to absorb new and alternate ways of thinking.

Managing this fine line effectively is an expectation of today's incoming talent for . . . well, everyone. Today, respect is not given solely because of the demographics we can easily put on paper—age, level, role—but is given for what you authentically contribute every day. Where simply being in a leadership position or having tenure once garnered respect, today it is compounded with an expectation to be transparent, vulnerable, and open to others' thoughts. While this may seem disrespectful, preposterous, or even dangerous, in this chapter I will explain how these behaviors will continue to grow and can be used to everyone's advantage.

One Coin, Two Sides Model: Authority Problem or Respect Redefined?

For this particular stereotype, the observable behavior is that millennials question or challenge people equally. Whether they feel comfortable to voice new ideas, challenge others' thoughts, or skirt the chain of command to meet a need, modern talent acts as though level or tenure are not too relevant. From a traditional perspective, this can be perceived as not having respect, or as lacking a sense of decorum for hierarchy, tenure, or elders in general. From a modern, top talent perspective, they are redefining respect to focus on experience and a concept I call "coversity," not simply on time served. They are acting from a broader mindset concerning equality. Table 6.1 summarizes the observable behavior, the two sides, and the supporting beliefs.

Exploring the Traditional Interpretation: Authority Issues

Some scenarios that are perceived as disrespectful to authority occur when younger talent:

> Invite leaders to lunch or to coffee just to get to know them

> Speak to leaders without the knowledge or interference of their manager. For example, after asking their manager about

Table 6.1   One Coin, Two Sides model for authority issues vs. redefining respect interpretation of modern behavior.

One Coin: One Observable Behavior	
Questioning or challenging people equally, regardless of tenure or level.	
Side 1: Traditional Interpretation	**Side 2: Top Talent, Millennial-Based Modern Interpretation**
Authority issues; disrespectful; lack a sense of decorum	Redefining respect
Supporting Beliefs:	**Supporting Beliefs:**
❭ There are some things you just don't do. There is a hierarchy or chain of command that should be respected.	❭ A real leader should recognize that the source of the challenge or new idea doesn't matter: young, old, male, female, etc. Challenging isn't a threat; I'm showing you that you have engaged me enough to want to suggest an idea or ask a question.
❭ I shouldn't have to prove myself to a younger person. In fact, I shouldn't be challenged at all.	
❭ Because I'm at the top, I shouldn't have to change to meet your needs; you should have to change to meet mine. If you have a particular way of communicating or working because you aren't similar to me, it's your job to adapt to my style.	❭ Everybody has something to teach someone else. We all should be respected and feel comfortable bringing our diverse thoughts and experiences to the table.
	❭ You hired me for me: my style, my way of thinking.
❭ Getting to the top took more grit and necessary navigation of the workplace that the younger generation dismisses. Knowledge and experience are not interchangeable. Knowledge can often be Googled, but situational leadership cannot.	❭ If you are threatened by having to justify your position, it makes me think you have something to hide or your position isn't that strong in the first place.
	❭ Transparent, collaborative leaders lead more profitable, engaged, happy workplaces. My way or the highway is a dinosaur approach that leads to unproductivity and disengagement.
❭ We have made great strides in embracing diversity already in the not so distant past. Millennials don't know how good they have it!	❭ I'm not sure I understand the value of deep experience in an age where it seems like everything is Google-able and changes very fast. The knowledge a tenured person has may be outdated.

Source: Invati Consulting

promotion guidelines and not getting a good answer, going directly to the one-up or two-up manager to discuss.

❭ Suggest ideas openly to leaders or more tenured individuals, especially when no feedback was requested. For example, at the end of a town hall meeting, when open for Q&A, someone who has only been with the company for a month asks a tough question.

> Expect a conversation that results in compromise when it comes to desired work and communication styles

> Do not assume they will have to assimilate to the existing culture

> Question leaders' or more tenured individuals' offered advice, approach, or opinions. This can often sound like, "But isn't it true that . . ." or "Things should be this way . . ." or fact-checking rather than taking the individual's word for it.

From a traditional perspective, growing up and throughout adulthood, giving respect was based in a command and control world. A few figures held the keys to shaping strategy in the workplace and for society at large. Communication was controlled more tightly by these same figures. The common saying at the time exemplifies the leadership environment: "When I say jump, you ask how high." We respected leaders solely because they were at the top. Some of those leaders may have been the underdog and gotten there through grit and determination. Some leaders may have been given their role through family ties or the "who you know" network. Regardless of their path, they were at the top and therefore deserved respect. Leaders and tenured individuals had power—the power of position, the power of influence, the power of knowledge. That meant that they did not need to prove themselves or change their style. Servant leadership wasn't yet an existing concept.

Boomers, as they came of age, rocked these concepts significantly. Let's take a brief journey through the evolution of management styles over the last century.

Recall that our current work structure primarily emerged post–Industrial Revolution and mass manufacturing. As national and multinational corporations evolved, something had to be done that hadn't been done before: manage processes and people at larger and larger scales, across larger distances. The manager role evolved to keep step, as did experimental styles of management.

In the early and mid-1900s, the focus was on numbers that defined profit and productivity, also known as "scientific management." Scientific management has evolved into a variety of work management practices today. To put it simply, at the time, work was divided into small, easily controlled tasks, where no single frontline employee knew the big picture of how all the pieces fit together. The big picture was knowledge limited to the manager's role. In corporate workplaces, there was a significant distinction between those who attended college and those who did not. At this time, it was common for leaders and managers to withhold information and to strictly control strategy—there was no reason or incentive for everyone to be involved. If anything, it was seen as a threat. Information was on a "need to know" basis. In this world, there was no room for everyone challenging everyone else—it was mostly characterized by the lower levels grumbling to themselves or through unions or other groups. To get to strategic levels was a clear privilege.

But after some time, as organizational development studies evolved, it became apparent that people's productivity was not solely governed by numbers. Precise measurements of movement to get tasks done and segmenting tasks down to the "dummy-can-do-it" level made people less productive than if they had autonomy and creativity. At the end of the day, the people closest to the work were more apt to understand ways to improve it, in contrast to the managers and leaders who were further removed. In the US, since the 1960s, young boomer managers and leaders began to experiment with managing styles that empower employees. As more millennials and generation Z join the workplace, the influence of the Internet continues to push for open management styles instead of the traditional command and control style.

In addition to the historical command and control management style, as mentioned in chapter 1, diversity in the workplace has changed significantly throughout recent history. Older generations grew up (both in childhood and in the workplace) in an environment surrounded by others who were more often similar to them than not. Immigrants and females were expected to "assimilate" in the workplace and respect was given accordingly—those that did a great job of assimilating were more likely to be noticed and recognized. For example, women who entered male-dominated workplaces in droves often changed their style to mirror the style of men in order to succeed. Art Kleiner, in his book *The Age of Heretics*, explains the gap and reigning mindset of those times: "In the back of their minds, the managers who hired these people no doubt expected them to be grateful—for these were groundbreaking efforts. Like immigrants, the increasing black and women staff were expected to dig in, work hard, find ways to assimilate, and gradually melt into the existing ambience of the company. In other words, as all immigrants found wherever they settle, the game was rigged against them. The hard part was learning to assimilate the constant belittling of their identity: 'Stop moving your hands that way. Stop making those kinds of jokes. Dress like the CEO dresses. Act like the finance manager acts.' When everyone comes from a similar culture, these restraints are learned from childhood, but for women and members of ethnic minorities, corporate culture was thoroughly alien. They would become aware, as only an outsider would become aware, of every slight detail of the prevailing ambiance of the white male organizational culture."[1]

It's only recently that significant changes have occurred. It was just in the 1960s and 1970s that many gender- and race-related issues came to the forefront and affirmative action began to emerge. Considering how recent these changes are and that most leaders today are of the older generation, the natural tendency is discomfort with diversity. An Ernst & Young study in 2013 supports this conclusion. When comparing all three generations, boomers received the lowest scores by all generations, including ratings shared by fellow boomers, with only 12 percent saying boomers are the best at "diversity" and 16 percent at "inclusive" leadership skills.[2] It is this type of approach that leads many corporate cultures, especially as one gets higher up, to feel like an old boys' club. Those that ask, "Why do we need to pander to young people's expectations?" are clearly a part of the command and control perspective and less likely to exhibit inclusive leadership styles.

In summary, in the past, the perceived tie between increased profits, increased productivity, and a sharply hierarchical structure was much clearer than today. There was also a difference in diversity that affected hierarchy, where work that received recognition was more narrowly limited by ethnicity and gender. The gap between college educated (managers and leaders) and non-college educated (frontline workers) was much more evident across industries as well. For all these reasons, the older perspective is that one should not expect leadership or tenured individuals to flex their approach and answer challenges. One should respect the chain of command when meeting needs and accept the answer "no" when a superior tells you. What other beliefs and societal norms do you feel influenced this perception of hierarchy and respect?

Exploring the Modern Interpretation: Respect Redefined

In stark contrast, millennials grew up in a time of transparency, equality, and globalization, all furthered exponentially by the advent of digital technology. In a rapidly evolving world of highly cognitive work and innovation/strategic goals, it's more beneficial than ever to promote idea flow and knowledge sharing among all levels and roles. In fact, the very notion of diversity is changing and therefore, we must reexamine our concepts of hierarchy, respect, and equality in the workplace.

For millennials, there wasn't a time when we didn't know what was happening behind closed doors. A lot happened to affect our opinion of leaders and those in power. Events in US history were all transparently shared, including the Monica Lewinsky and Enron scandals, the housing bubble, and more. The advent of cable television, followed by the Internet, increased access to world events and leaders like never before, and in turn, increased expectations of transparency, feelings of mistrust, and questioning of authority in all generations. As a result, millennials don't share in older generations' tendency to respect elders solely for age and tenure. We ask for proof from people who thought they no longer would have to provide that proof. If a leader or tenured individual is threatened by having to explain an opinion or approach, it may be perceived as having something to hide, or as having a weak argument to begin with.

In addition to trust issues, millennials have grown up in a time where diversity is so constantly present, where the majority is the minority, where learning about cultures around the globe is highly accessible, that *they assume diversity exists everywhere and have a decreased barrier to accepting macro-differences.* When we grew up, because of digital technology, we were constantly surrounded by alternative ways of thinking and people challenging one another, regardless of who was an actual off-line expert. The Internet is the great equalizer. We have grown up watching emerging voices, many who were initially anonymous, gain followings and make an impact, only to find out later what they looked like, their age, gender, and so on.

Consider the example of a friend of mine. He was a teenager who loved watching World Wrestling Federation (WWF) in high school. He wanted to make some side money, so he assigned himself an official e-mail address of a journalist at a WWF reporting website. He started writing articles, gained a following, and got paid for a few months before the website realized he was a teenager! His age didn't matter to his followers though. They respected his voice. This example showcases how powerful the Internet has truly been: it has removed the innate barriers we have to judge people by the characteristics we can see (ethnicity, gender, age, etc.) and instead allows us to focus on everything below the surface.

Top talent millennials do respect tenure and age, but they also have a broader view of respect that includes valuing all perspectives regardless of characteristics like age, ethnicity, and gender. As *Time* magazine's political columnist, Joe Klein, says, "Diversity has been written into the DNA of American life; any institution that lacks a rainbow array has come to seem diminished, if not diseased." Modern talent assumes that macro-diversity exists and is embraced in the workplace. If it doesn't exist, they automatically sense the unproductive, disengaging, unattractive old boys' club and focus on other workplaces instead.

With this lens in mind, respect as defined by millennials and generations beyond is based on authentic transparency and leadership that isn't what I call a "pale, male, and stale mindset" but reflects the broad diversity represented by consumers and talent. We expect these leaders to be promoted based on micro-differences in strengths and weaknesses and real experience, rather than favorites and tenure. While millennials and later generations may need to be coached on the value of time-built expertise, a balance should be struck and diverse, alternative ways of thinking encouraged. Because the influence and reach of the Internet is global, this shift in definition is global as well. Modern talent asks questions and voices thoughts to leaders and tenured individuals just as they would a peer.

Leveraging a Broader Definition of Respect to Build a Modern Organization

Where respect was once given based on level, tenure, and age, respect is given today for ongoing authentic contributions that stand out. In essence, respect is not given by millennials to roles or positions, but to actions and behaviors regardless of position. Many organizations are experimenting with new structures, such as flat or circular organizations (the so-called "holacracy" championed by the online shoe and clothing outlet Zappos, where individuals are managed through peer-to-peer relationships instead of hierarchy). Before pursuing these larger changes, there are three fundamental interventions to consider: promoting coversity, attitudes, and social media presence.

Modern talent holds the belief that *the best workplaces are successful because they embrace people's micro-differences. They are more innovative, more creative, more able to serve their customers when they do not try to put people in boxes based on macro-differences or when they do not have too many similar people in the workplace.* To embrace micro-differences, there is a need for another critical shift in the workplace. Instead of focusing on embracing diversity through diversity training and affinity networks, I encourage focusing on creating a culture based on a new concept I coined: coversity. Coversity programs are those that intentionally bring diverse people together around a common challenge or topic to explore their differences and enable acceptance.

In contrast, diversity programs, as we have traditionally defined them, focus on dividing people to create silos of support based on their macro-differences: those traits we can see such as age, ethnicity, and gender. In other words, putting people into boxes. The very term "diversity" is divisive and comes from the latin verb *diverte*, which meant "to turn aside" and eventually evolved to mean "separate." Diversity promotes isolating people by identifying separate groups: the women's network (are men allowed?), the millennial network, the Working with India (or other country) cultural training, and so on. It's based on the idea that by putting together all the people who share the same macro-trait, they will somehow learn how to collaborate and assimilate with the people outside the network or training program.

If we are truly trying to create inclusive environments, what we need is coversity. The prefix "co-" implies togetherness, partnership, equality. Combined with "-versity," it implies that, while we are different, we are equal and we can partner together. Instead of a millennial network, it's having a generations network, where people of all generations can come together and *converse, connect,* and *collaborate.*

Is there a benefit to gaining support from like-minded people? Absolutely. Inside of the coverse, there are like-minded people who may group together to create themes and patterns to explore. But deciding where the divisions start, at what level, is critical. Currently, because the first level of division is the macro-difference, we have little to no time or space to share what we learn to those outside the network. When I was part of an Asian network, one of the goals that made the network worthwhile was the support and ability to confide in other Asians. However, what was equally important was the ability to share Asian culture with non-Asians and to create acceptance around differences in recognition methods, feedback skills, work ethic, leadership skills, and so on. Although it may have even been a part of my work plan that I was a participant in the network, it wasn't on my Caucasian colleague's work plan. As a result, there wasn't a priority for him to understand how to work with me. A joint ethnicity coversity group would have been much more useful, where we could have openly discussed recognition methods and the other topics. Then, we could have had subgroups for individual support.

Consider having a gender network, where people can talk about gender-related issues together. I once encountered a women's network that had developed an extraordinary leadership program. It was done so well that men started attending just to get the same training! Let's put the focus on the common topics both sides struggle with. Currently the champions of women in the workplace say the biggest challenge is bringing men into the conversation. That's understandably difficult when you blatantly call something a women's network (basically putting up a "no boys allowed" sign!). Within a gender network, on the other hand, subgroups for women or men or transgender individuals can exist for support.

In addition to networks, the idea of coversity can be applied to formal diversity training. For example, it is much more effective to have an unconscious bias training instead of groups like Working with India or China or South America and so on. Unconscious bias addresses the overarching behavior gap of acting on biases we hold that we aren't consciously aware of. These biases may conflict with our conscious values and, by bringing these biases to the conscious level, we can change our action. Because we are training at the topic level, we are promoting coversity. Again, it is still important to understand the specific cultural norms of a country. In this example, that would look like learning about unconscious bias, followed by specific, shorter training on cultural norms of a country. But giving a training without that context promotes the idea that everyone from that country is exactly the same and promotes a negative, silo-based version of embracing diversity.

Coversity is about exploring together the differences in perspective, experiences, thought, communication style, strengths and weaknesses. The goal of building a coverse is to bring to life the traits below the surface. From a millennial perspective, that is how things are organized on the Internet—dividing people by topics and interests instead of physical traits. It's what we are used to. The Internet removed the human barrier of judgment based on macro-diversity. What conversations are we missing out on because we promote diversity instead of coversity?

In addition to building coversity through new affinity networks and training programs, leaders, managers, and tenured individuals need to shift their concept of respect. Consider the following changes to redefine respect in the modern world:

> **It's not personal, it's engaging.** It is important to recognize that the act of asking a question *is not personal.* It's not a personal attack on your position, your level, your expertise. Rather, *you have said something that made them want to engage, learn more, or contribute to your thought.*

> **It's a challenge to improve your management capability.** If you are a manager, and someone circumvents the chain of command because they weren't satisfied with your answer, it is a sign that *you need to give better answers.* (It may be a hard truth to swallow!) You may not be used to providing detailed answers or coaching into softer areas like career development or team collaboration. Yet that is a primary focus for enabling employees to get everyday work done in our strategic, highly cognitive environment. If you don't have the ability to communicate well when asked questions in these arenas, individuals who report to you become disengaged enough to want to go over your head.

> **It's an enabler.** If you are a manager, and someone simply seeks out leaders to get to know them, you should *encourage it.* Accelerating one's knowledge of the business's strategy, relationships, and culture can only help one become more productive and engaged.

> **Stop assimilating. Start growing.** Lastly, do not shy away from different cultural (ethnic, gender, age, etc.) ways of thinking. *It's okay for everyone to stop assimilating.* As we learned from Alex Pentland, the best work comes from consciously finding and integrating new ideas. To be an effective leader, embrace the possibilities offered by integrating new ways of thinking into your honed expertise.

Thirdly, along with building coversity and shifting attitudes, the next step to embracing the new definition of respect is to start authentically and transparently contributing. Where businesses were once local, they are now global. Where businesses once controlled their image, the perception is now crowdsourced via social media. A connected, transparent, socially accessible leader garners respect more easily than the invisible, command and control, behind closed doors leader. Similarly, for tenured individual and managers, there are benefits to being more transparent.

This doesn't necessarily mean having thousands of followers on Twitter or spending hours on social media. *The Social CEO* study found that "many CEOs who don't participate in social media are actually communicating with employees through company intranets (50 percent) and making themselves visible to external constituents on their company websites (62 percent). We find that CEOs are finding ways to be social without being active on Facebook, Twitter and LinkedIn."[3] Whether you are the CEO or the company subject matter expert, it's not necessarily the tools you use that are important in this case. What's important is that you are using something and that it is *you* who is using it. Many leaders have PR teams crafting messages for them. This is the very definition of inauthenticity and greatly takes away from the impact of a vulnerable message.

Consider sharing thoughts on the following topics:

> Openly sharing strategy justification, meaning, and impact

> Asking for feedback through questions

> Sharing your personal challenges and your ways to overcome them

> Sharing how you became an expert and why it is important to you or a passion of yours

By communicating transparently, you empower others on their own journeys, you inspire others, and you gain their respect through good old-fashioned honesty. *The Social CEO* highlighted the many benefits executives have found by their CEO's participation in social media. The report states that 78 percent found that participation has a positive impact on company reputation, 75 percent say it is a good way to communicate with employees, 64 percent say it helps to find and attract new customers, and 72 percent say it keeps the CEO in touch with what's happening inside the company.[4]

In summary, the key intervention here is to kill the concept of the old boys' club and leadership solely based on command and control. The world is too diverse, too cognitive, and too transparent today to tolerate it. The idea that someone, as a leader, feels most comfortable conversing and practicing in pale, male, and stale environments where their years of building political, bureaucratic relationships prevails is against all ideals of what makes a leader effective today. An effective leader today is someone who can break down superficial, visible barriers such as gender, race, and age and connect deeply with their audience, be it consumers or employees. *It's okay if employees talk to leaders more openly and directly; in fact, it may be a key part of keeping leaders agile and able to make effective decisions.* Similarly, tenured individuals need to be able to apply their expertise across a large and diverse organization. Being open to alternative ways of thinking helps one be agile and open to coaching and working with a diverse range of people. By shifting culture toward coversity, attitudes toward respect, and practices toward transparent contribution, we can embrace and leverage the modern expectation of building a culture that has authentic respect for every individual.

Tales from the Trenches

To learn more about what these ideas look like in practice, here is an example of a training and affinity network based on the concept of coversity and a story of a social CEO.

Case Study 6.1

Generation University: Building Coversity Culture for the Multi-Generation Work Environment

One of my flagship programs at Invati Consulting is Generation University (Gen U), a blended learning program designed to progressively build collaboration skills across generations and create a cultural movement around embracing different generations in the workplace. The results of the program have been astounding, as exemplified by one of our clients, the University of the Pacific. An extraordinary 100 percent of the participants reported improvements in productivity, engagement, and working relationships, signifying an experience that went beyond training and into developing capabilities that drove measurable business impact and culture change!

The University of the Pacific had been experiencing relatively common issues with their multi-generation work environment. There had been significantly increased turnover with younger, new staff who felt older management was shutting down their ideas and not tapping into their talent. Tenured employees had highlighted the need to learn collaboration skills, what motivates millennials, and how to overcome biases. As stated later by a gen X participant from the pilot program, "I think there is a lot of prejudice against this generation [millennials] on campus and it became really evident after I took the class and noticed certain terms and stereotypes in place in my workplace and other spaces on campus."

To address these issues, Generation University was a clear winner to create coversity. While most generational training programs focus on sharing content about birth date ranges and data-unsupported attitudes and values, Gen U followed many of the principles and concepts in this book. It focused on creating conversations, attitude shifts, and understanding between members of all generations, supported by providing a new lens on each generation. The results are a training program that doesn't just teach participants how to work across generations, but provides them with tools to embrace macro-diversity as well. As a participant stated at the close of the course: "From the course work, I have learned that many of the assumptions our society makes about generations are based on fiction, not facts. Instead, people are likely to act the way they do because of environmental factors. For this reason, it is important that we know persons on an individual level instead of relying on stereotypes."

Gen U created a powerful cultural change by:

❖ Alleviating the focus on "fixing" or "working with" any one generation

❖ Sharing broader context and implications of influential events and environment as it pertains across all generations

❖ Realizing that the trainers do not hold the answers for collaboration—the participants do

❖ Focusing on creating a safe environment for people to talk about their micro-differences

By shifting the approach to building coversity by bringing together diverse participants to converse on common challenges, the training program was much more powerful than a traditional diversity training.

Case Study 6.2

Building Respect (Among Many Other Benefits) Through Social Media

One of the best examples of effective social media use is the CEO Richard Branson and Virgin, his UK-based entertainment, music, and travel services conglomerate. His cultivation of transparency and authenticity has led to a highly engaged community of 9.5 million followers on LinkedIn and 8.2 million on Twitter, not to mention 7,000+ shares of each of his blog posts on Virgin's main site. Nearly 43,000 of Virgin's 50,000+ current employees are on LinkedIn as well. Virgin's subsidiaries consistently rank on global and regional best places to work surveys and overall reported revenues of £15 billion in 2012. Clearly, Branson's approach of staying in touch and being transparent has aided in his success. For our final case study, we highlight the elements that make his social media approach work.

❖ **Authenticity.** Branson most often posts to social media himself, including personal pictures; he doesn't rely on marketing teams to craft his content. By being the owner of his message, instead of letting someone else speak for him, Branson establishes trust.

❖ **Vulnerability.** Branson shares on the Virgin blog, "I enjoy reading through my social media feeds. It's a great way to get feedback about our goods and services, and a wonderful way to find inspiration for new ideas."[5] Branson has realized that the power of social media is to challenge him and his company. Without both positive and negative feedback, Virgin can't improve. The focus is on growth, not the status quo.

❖ **Cascaded culture.** "Richard tweets and blogs 24/7 every day, so it's knitted into the fabric of the whole company now," says Virgin's content manager Greg Rose.[6] Because of Branson's role modeling, the culture throughout is transparent and open to feedback.

By using social media as a tool for increased transparency and taking in feedback, no matter what the source, Virgin has built a culture that is respected and recognized by modern talent globally. Branson has integrated both the attitudes and actions that create a road to genuine trust and respect. With the role modeling of the CEO, all individuals, including managers and tenured individuals, participate in creating a culture that's transparent, open to feedback, and open to micro-differences.

Summary: From Authority Problems to Embracing Coversity

In this chapter, we learned that millennials skirt hierarchy and treat relationships more equally than previous generations. Millennials believe micro-differences (the differences below the surface) matter more than macro-differences such as age, gender, and race. The nature of digital technology has created new rules for who is respected based on ongoing authentic contribution and grit instead of age, level, tenure, or other accolades. Instead of feeling threatened, those with tenure and leadership roles can use this level of feedback to continue to personally grow and influence others.

To leverage the power of micro-differences, we found that even before experimenting with brand new organizational structures, other changes can be made. We talked about embracing the concept of "coversity," in which people are brought together by topic and can then further subdivide based on macro-differences, or our traditional concept of diversity. Coversity helps us bring together people who are different to converse, connect, collaborate, and ultimately generate new ways of thinking. It enables us to consider that we can be different, but equal—we don't have to be mired in an us vs. them mentality, but instead focus on how there are differences on an individual level. We shared stories of women's networks, Asian networks, and unconscious bias training as examples.

We also talked about attitude shifts for tenured individuals or those in leadership positions. These attitude shifts range from not taking questions or challenges personally to embracing opportunities to stay in touch while growing established expertise. Lastly, we discovered that social media is a new way to establish transparency and "relatability" and gain feedback in the large, multinational organizations of today, whether used internally with employees or externally with customers.

Through our examples of Generation University and Virgin's use of social media, we saw the power of embracing a new idea of respect, based on openness instead of hierarchy. In a time of rapid change, if you stayed with what served you well in the past you could fail easily. Having millennials challenge you with their natural tendency to respect everyone equally is actually a gift. Like each of the other four stereotypes we discussed, it's possible to view and harness this trait as a strength—it's just a matter of what lens you choose to look through.

How Modern Is Your Culture?

How well do you think your organization is meeting modern talent needs? Read each statement and place an X in the appropriate column, then sum up your score. We have stated "my company" for the focus of each statement, but feel free to replace with "my immediate work group" or another community if it serves your purpose better. The assessment can also be found online at themillennialmyth.com/resources, where you can compare your answers with other readers.

	Strongly Disagree	Disagree	Neutral	Agree	Strongly Agree
My company's leadership doesn't just disseminate information to the employees; feedback is welcome from everyone.					
My company's management and culture create a sense of respect for everyone's skills.					
My company's managers act as collaborative partners with their direct reports.					
Employees can build a relationship with company leaders if they choose.					
I trust my coworkers.					
My company culture feels like it embraces all individuals.					
My company culture does not feel like it is working in silos.					
Most people in my company are open to changing their communication and perspective, rather than assuming everyone will assimilate to them.					
My company culture does not feel like an "old boys' club."					
Total number of X's in each column:					

If the majority of your X's fall in the strongly disagree or disagree columns, your organization is leaning toward a traditional perspective that is at risk of disengaging modern talent. You may want to see where you can make some changes through reviewing portions of this chapter, trying the 10-Minute Champion ideas below, investigating our online resources, or reaching out to us for further help.

10-Minute Champion

What can you do to shift your organization toward a modern culture? Consider championing the following ideas in your work group, intended to take no more than 10 minutes each.

- ☐ **Reverse mentoring.** Consider something you are about to do. Ask a lower level or, conversely, a tenured employee to give you feedback on the idea or approach. For a more in-depth initiative, consider championing a reverse mentoring lunch 'n' learn. Pair tenured individuals with less tenured individuals. Ask tenured individuals to share a current challenge and get feedback from their partner. Rotate after a set time.

- ☐ **Appreciate micro-differences.** The next time someone has a differing work style or point of view than you, spend 10 minutes discussing where their style or point of view came from. Intentionally try to put on their lens by asking questions like "How has this style worked for you in the past?" or "What experiences have led you to believe this point of view?" The tone should be curious and collaborative rather than confrontational.

- ☐ **Create a coversity conversation.** Create your own coversity group by discussing a 10-minute, interest-based topic around lunch where everyone can voice ideas. Topics could be gender relations, leadership styles, introvert/extrovert/ambivert, or anything that's relevant to your particular work environment.

☐ **Build a social media presence.** Whatever your company's social media presence is today, consider duplicating it. This could mean a Twitter account, where you spend 10 minutes crafting an insightful tweet, or a LinkedIn account, where you contribute regularly to a LinkedIn group. It could be an internal network such as a subject matter expert group. Challenge yourself to post insights about your work, challenges you are having, and resources you find.

☐ **Create your own idea.** Feel free to create your own ideas about creating connections between individuals, regardless of macro-differences.

Add your idea and view others' ideas on the 10-Minute Champion at themillennialmyth.com/resources

A Millennial-Inspired Modern World

We live in an age of heretics: an age where unconventional ideas become conventional wisdom rapidly. And that's a good thing, because the future of industrial society depends on our ability to transcend the destructive management of the past and build a better kind of business.

—Art Kleiner, *The Age of Heretics*

What if we could change the autocomplete in our heads related to millennials? What if there was more to the story of the multi-generation workplace than endless divisive blogs, top 10 lists, and white papers? Instead, what if we all acknowledged and embraced the momentous difference digital technology has created? What workplace could we create together?

The results on search engines may not change, but our approach certainly can. Throughout our journey of transforming these five millennial myths into workplace breakthroughs, some of the concepts discussed may sound unorthodox or heretical. Many organizations are just at the beginning of cultural transformation in response to the advent of digital technology. Despite the continual rise of the knowledge worker over the last 60 years, we haven't done enough to question "how we've always done things" and redefine effectiveness in organizations.

Picture an employee hard at work. Surrounded by beige and gray walls, beams of light from fluorescent ceiling bulbs and backlit LED monitors collide 12 inches away from their face. A document is drawn up and while typing away, dings from incoming e-mails and instant messages abound. Every decision feels vital, but having all the relevant information seems impossible. The phone next to their arm buzzes with an incoming message. Filtering through all the data and noise to understand what's important is a constant battle. Their hand looks permanently claw-shaped from mouse and smartphone usage. Voices are everywhere. They walk to the nearest window to take a break, about three minutes away. As the workday ends, they contemplate the myriad of errands and tasks awaiting at home. There is an evening virtual meeting with global partners and a few more e-mails to get through before going to bed for a six-hour nap. Their work relies on an increasing number of connections to people they may have never seen or hardly know.

Throughout it all, there is an innate desire to contribute, to do something of meaning, to pursue excellence, to have a positive impact, to meet personal goals. Our employee is in an environment that is more egalitarian, more diverse, more global than before. What would a reinvented workplace look like in this world that enables engagement and productivity?

Picture another employee. After sleeping a full eight hours, this employee takes the time at home to eat breakfast and create a prioritized list of focused items for the day. This employee has experimented with personal productivity and decided not to check their phone for e-mails until later. They arrive at work, and as they walk to their work area, they pass by small teams and collaboration spaces that bring the outside in, but with minimal distractions. No one feels the need to wear headphones, and there are spaces to make phone calls just a short walk away. At their desk, there are a few notes from other team members. The employee picks the hardest thing to do on their list and starts with that task. When they find they don't know something, they go online to the intranet and find a highly rated video posted by another employee on an easily searchable discussion forum. The employee has planned for a five-hour workday in the office today and then they are going to go home to manage their other errands. After completing the toughest task in the first three hours with minimal distractions, they open their e-mails and spend an hour managing those. The employee has a meeting with a clearly defined objective over lunch in a fun collaboration space where their teammate is white-boarding ideas with a sandwich in hand. After leaving well before rush hour traffic, running some errands, and pursuing a mental break, later in the evening they spend a moment synthesizing and reflecting on the major task of the day. The employee creates a write-up for their manager and hits send. They go to sleep, knowing they've accomplished something for a role they enjoy, for a company they have chosen to work for.

This workplace is different from the one we are used to seeing today. It is flexible to personal productivity through hours and work environment. It fosters connections between people of all levels and all backgrounds in the most efficient routes possible. Ideas flow and are cultivated organically through the organization. It is an environment of ongoing learning and feedback, where employees feel connected to the overall business mission as though they are business owners. And finally, that overall business mission is one that benefits society at large in some way, outside of a sole focus on corporate profits.

Ultimately, these are the types of changes that millennial behavior shows us are important for the workplace. By growing up in a world of digital technology, these are the inherent expectations and trends millennials globally are bringing to the table that will have an impact for generations to come. And rightfully so, because digital is not going away. New expectations of employees and of customers and of society in general aren't going away either. Millennials, instead of a danger, are really a reflection of the society in which they grew up in, and in which all of us now live.

If these expectations and trends are ignored for the sake of holding onto the status quo, we will continue to witness the trends we have already been experiencing. Higher turnover based on a lack of trust between employers and employees. Disengagement and burnout due to lack of understanding of productivity in a digital, strategic work world. Lack of innovation and creativity stifling growth, eventually leading to "Uber-izing" of companies as competitors disrupt the scene.

In Table C.1, I've highlighted each of the myths, the transformations in perspective to the new language, and the related organizational changes we discussed. Keep in mind our guiding principles as you continue your journey. When you meet a millennial, consider their behavior not as a fleeting generational trait, but a sign of what's modern and what's to come. Recall that just as every coin has two sides, every behavior can be interpreted multiple ways. It's your prerogative to step back and evaluate which interpretation you choose to act on. Recall that our research pertained to top talent around the globe and doesn't necessarily apply to every millennial. Your own experience, conversations, and interpretations are just as important to understanding modern employees. The interpretations, organizational changes, and case studies are just the beginning for experimentation with creating the modern workplace. Lastly, recall that a foundation of trust and respect are at the root of every strong relationship. And what is a company if not a multitude of relationships seeking to achieve a mutual goal?

Take a look at your scores from the end of chapter assessments. Depending on your overall score, give yourself an estimate. How far away is this future of work for your organization? Five years? Ten years? Twenty-five years? What help do you need to move forward on the journey? Recall the resources we have posted on our resource library at themillennialmyth.com/resources, including the one-page guides, the co-created key quotes document, the 10-Minute Champion ideas, and the online version of the assessment and associated results.

Certainly, my research is ongoing and has much more room for discovery. Each of the major concepts shared has a wealth of room for experimentation and research in the future. Another key area, for example, is identifying what lessons, attitudes, and best practices we should

Table C.1 Summary of the five millennial myths transformed into workplace breakthroughs.

1. From Lazy	To Productivity Redefined	Related Org Changes
Because: Traditional mindset Work structure based in mass manufacturing world Belief that there's only one way best work can be achieved	Because: Modern Mindset Digital, highly cognitive tasks require more flexibility for productivity	❭ Flexibility in work hours ❭ Flexibility in work location ❭ Goal-oriented instead of process-oriented work approach
2. From Entitled	**To Entrepreneurial**	**Related Org Changes**
Because: Traditional mindset Promotion, flexibility, challenging work, access to leaders, and more were seen as benefits or privileges, not base expectations	Because: Modern Mindset Digital technology has created new skills and expectations that align with an entrepreneurial mindset: fast-paced, high growth, business ownership, mission-based work.	❭ Challenging work plans ❭ Build intrapreneurship culture where idea flow is encouraged throughout the organization
3. From Needing to be Hand-held	**To Agile**	**Related Org Changes**
Because: Traditional mindset Pace of work and change used to be slower Amount of information was less We didn't get rewards just for showing up	Because: Modern Mindset More information to filter through Less time to develop and adapt to changes More feedback enables agility	❭ Create a culture of ongoing meaningful feedback where feedback is disconnected from performance management ❭ Better learning and development department strategies that serve inside and outside the classroom
4. From Disloyal	**To Empowered to Impact**	**Related Org Changes**
Because: Traditional mindset It was possible to stay at one company lifelong	Because: Modern Mindset Time of instability and mistrust Loyalty must be earned by employer Seek purpose Caring for the community is a sign of caring for employees	❭ Social responsibility programs that tie into more than just financial contribution ❭ Clear mission and vision that includes benefit to society ❭ Every employee can connect their role back to social impact

More ▶

Table C.1   Summary of the five millennial myths transformed into workplace breakthroughs (*continued*).

5. From Authority Issues	To Respect Redefined	Related Org Changes
Because: Traditional mindset Command and control structure	Because: Modern Mindset Collaborative structure based on micro-diversity, where age, level, and tenure are only some of the traits that earn respect	› Evolving the concept of embracing diversity to building coversity › Increased transparency and openness to feedback as attitude shifts › Social media as a possible tool to embrace

Source: Invati Consulting

strive to bring forward from before the advent of digital technology. What adaptations and lessons should we teach millennials and gen Z as they enter the workplace?

With ideas in hand like building coversity networks, using virtual platforms to encourage idea flow and learning, instituting flexible work environments, and doing authentic social good in your local communities, I hope you find yourself empowered. When you started this journey, you may have had a different language for describing millennials, but I hope to have shown you a new way of thinking about millennials and modern talent, based on the radically different world in which we live today—a world that has deeply influenced this generation and will continue to influence society at large. As we embark on the journey of disrupting the workplace, a greater momentum of champions of the modern workplace will emerge and shake the status quo, the way we've always done things.

Change is inevitable. Be one of those champions.

Notes

Preface

1. Samantha Lee and Shana Lebowitz, "20 Cognitive Biases That Screw Up Your Decisions," *Business Insider*, August 26, 2015, accessed July 24, 2016, http://www.businessinsider.com/cognitive-biases-that-affect-decisions -2015-8.

Introduction

1. Neil Howe and William A. Strauss, *Millennials Rising: The Next Great Generation* (New York: Vintage Books, 2000).

2. Carroll Doherty, Jocelyn Kiley, and Bridget Jameson, *Most Millennials Resist the "Millennial" Label*, Pew Research Center, September 3, 2015, http://www.people-press.org/files/2015/09/09-03-2015-Generations -release.pdf.

3. Amy Adkins, "What Millennials Want From Work and Life," Gallup Business Journal, May 11, 2016, accessed July 24, 2016, http://www.gallup .com/businessjournal/191435/millennials-work-life.aspx.

4. Dan Schawbel, "The Cost of Millennial Retention Study," Millennial Branding, August 6, 2013, accessed July 24, 2016, http://millennialbranding.com/2013/cost-millennial-retention-study/.

5. Adkins, "What Millennials Want From Work and Life."

6. Dan Schawbel, "The High School Careers Study," Millennial Branding, February 3, 2014, accessed July 24, 2016, http://millennialbranding.com /2014/high-school-careers-study/.

7. *GE Annual Report 2000*, accessed September 2, 2016, http://www.ge.com /annual00/download/images/GEannual00.pdf.

Chapter 1

1. Eric Hoover, "The Millennial Muddle: How Stereotyping Students Became a Thriving Industry and a Bundle of Contradictions," *Chronicle of Higher Education*, October 11, 2009, accessed July 24, 2016, http://chronicle.com /article/the_millennial_muddle_how/48772.

2. Paul Meshanko, "STADA Webinar: 12 Rules of Respect—The Neuroscience of Employee Engagement," YouTube, October 23, 2015, accessed July 24, 2016, https://youtu.be/vdvcWWgibVk.

3. Grace L. Williams, "Generation Z to Eclipse Millennials as Economic Force, Says Goldman Sachs," Today.com, December 4, 2014, accessed January 10, 2017, http://www.today.com/money/generation-z-eclipse -millennials-economic-force-says-goldman-sachs-t59436.

4. Eileen Patten and Richard Fry, "How Millennials Today Compare with Their Grandparents 50 Years Ago," Pew Research Center, March 19, 2015, accessed July 24, 2016, http://www.pewresearch.org/fact-tank/2015/03/19/ how-millennials-compare-with-their-grandparents/#!19; Richard Fry, "Millennials Overtake Baby Boomers as America's Largest Generation," Pew Research Center, April 25, 2016, accessed July 24, 2016, http://www.pewresearch.org/fact-tank/2016/04/25/millennials-overtake -baby-boomers/.

5. Fry, "Millennials Overtake Baby Boomers as America's Largest Generation."

6. Patten and Fry, "How Millennials Today Compare with Their Grandparents 50 Years Ago."

7. Ibid.

8. Gretchen Livingston, "Fewer than Half of US Kids Today Live in a 'Traditional' Family," Pew Research Center, December 22, 2014, accessed September 2, 2016, http://www.pewresearch.org/fact-tank/2014/12/22/less -than-half-of-u-s-kids-today-live-in-a-traditional-family/.

9. Patten and Fry, "How Millennials Today Compare with Their Grandparents 50 Years Ago."

10. "Table 330.10. Average Undergraduate Tuition and Fees and Room and Board Rates Charged for Full-time Students in Degree-Granting Postsec-ondary Institutions, by Level and Control of Institution: 1963–64 through 2012–13," National Center for Education Statistics, 2013, accessed October 12, 2016, https://nces.ed.gov/programs/digest/d13/tables/dt13 _330.10.asp.

11. Patten and Fry, "How Millennials Today Compare with Their Grandparents 50 Years Ago"; Livingston, "Fewer than Half of US Kids Today Live in a 'Traditional' Family"; "Table 330.10. Average Undergraduate Tuition and Fees and Room and Board Rates."

12. Hoover, "The Millennial Muddle."

13. Maximiliano Dvorkin, "Jobs Involving Routine Tasks Aren't Growing," Federal Reserve Bank of St. Louis, January 4, 2016, accessed September 2, 2016, https://www.stlouisfed.org/on-the-economy/2016/january/jobs -involving-routine-tasks-arent-growing.

14. Ibid.

Chapter 2

1. Dvorkin, "Jobs Involving Routine Tasks Aren't Growing."

2. Carl Frey and Michael Osborne, *The Future of Employment: How Susceptible Are Jobs to Computerisation?* Engineering Sciences, Oxford University, September 17, 2013, accessed July 24, 2016, http://www.oxfordmartin.ox.ac.uk/downloads/academic/The_Future_of _Employment.pdf.

3. *Global Generations: A Global Study on Work-Life Challenges Across Generations*, Ernst & Young, 2015, accessed July 24, 2016, http://www.ey.com/Publication/vwLUAssets/EY-global-generations-a -global-study-on-work-life-challenges-across-generations/$FILE/EY -global-generations-a-global-study-on-work-life-challenges-across -generations.pdf.

4. Brigid Schulte, "Millennials Want a Work-Life Balance. Their Bosses Just Don't Get Why," *Washington Post*, May 5, 2015, accessed July 24, 2016, https://www.washingtonpost.com/local/millennials-want-a-work-life -balance-their-bosses-just-dont-get-why/2015/05/05/1859369e-f376 -11e4-84a6-6d7c67c50db0_story.html.

5. Ibid.

6. Kim Jungsoo and Richard de Dear, "Workspace Satisfaction: The Privacy-Communication Trade-Off in Open-Plan Offices," *Journal of Environmental Psychology*, 2013, DOI:10.1016/j.jenvp.2013.06.007.

7. Andrew Simms, "The Four-Day Week: Less Is More," *Guardian*, February 22, 2013, accessed July 26, 2016, http://www.theguardian.com /money/2013/feb/22/four-day-week-less-is-more.

8. *Design Language for Place*, Microsoft, April 12, 2016, accessed September 2, 2016, http://microsoftworkplace.com/designlanguage/.

9. Jennifer Warnick, "Productivity by Design," Microsoft, accessed July 26, 2016, http://news.microsoft.com/stories/b16/.

Chapter 3

1. Stacey Ferreira and Jared Kleinert, *2 Billion Under 20: How Millennials Are Breaking Down Age Barriers and Changing the World* (New York, St. Martins Press, 2016).

2. Michael Grothaus, "Meet The Father-Son Team Making $1.3 Million On YouTube," Fast Company, May 4, 2015, accessed September 2, 2016, https://www.fastcompany.com/3045807/passion-to-profit/meet-the -father-son-team-making-13-million-on-youtube.

3. Tiare Dunlap, "This 10-Year-Old 'Kidpreneur' Invented the Only Candy to Be Served at This Year's White House Easter Egg Roll," *People*, March 26,

2016, accessed September 2, 2016, http://www.people.com/article
/zollidrops-alina-morse-10-year-old-invented-candy-served-white
-house-easter-egg-roll.

4. Larry Kim, "This 12-Year-Old CEO Runs a $150,000 Business," *Inc.*,
September 15, 2014, accessed September 2, 2016, http://www.inc.com/larry
-kim/this-12-year-old-ceo-runs-a-150k-business.html.

5. Edmund Sass, "American Educational History: A Hypertext Timeline,"
October 6, 2016, accessed October 17, 2016, http://www.eds-resources.com
/educationhistorytimeline.html.

6. Diane Shao, "Knocking on Opportunity's Door," *Science*, October 21, 2016,
accessed November 1, 2016, http://science.sciencemag.org/content/354
/6310/382.

7. Schawbel, "The High School Careers Study" (see introduction, n. 6).

8. *Millennials and the Future of Work*, Millennial Branding and oDesk, May
14, 2013, accessed July 26, 2016, http://www.slideshare.net/oDesk
/millennials-and-the-future-of-work-survey-results.

9. Josh Bersin, *Predictions for 2016: A Bold New World of Talent, Learning,
Leadership, and HR Technology Ahead*, Bersin by Deloitte, January 2016,
accessed July 26, 2016, http://marketing.bersin.com/predictions-for-2016
.html.

10. Alex Pentland, *Social Physics: How Good Ideas Spread—the Lessons from a
New Science* (New York, Penguin Group, 2014).

11. Alex Goryachev, *Cisco Ignites Companywide Startup Culture*, Cisco, June 9,
2016, accessed August 18, 2016, https://newsroom.cisco.com
/documents/10157/14740/790057-WhitePaper-060816-FINAL.pdf.

12. Ibid.

Chapter 4

1. Nicholas G. Carr, *The Shallows: What the Internet Is Doing to Our Brains*
(New York: W.W. Norton, 2010).

2. Karl Moore, "Agility: The Ingredient That Will Define Next Generation
Leadership," *Forbes*, June 12, 2012, accessed October 17, 2016,
http://www.forbes.com/sites/karlmoore/2012/06/12/agility-the-ingredient
-that-will-define-next-generation-leadership.

3. Todd Tauber and Temple Smolen, *How the Workforce Learns in 2016*,
degreed, 2016, accessed August 8, 2016, http://get.degreed.com/hubfs
/Degreed_How_the_Workforce_Learns_in_2016.pdf.

Chapter 5

1. *Workforce 2020 The Looming Talent Crisis*, SAP Success Factors, 2014, accessed August 8, 2016, https://www.successfactors.com/en_us/lp /workforce-2020-insights.html.

2. *Big Demands and High Expectations*, Deloitte, January 21, 2014, accessed August 10, 2016, https://www2.deloitte.com/al/en/pages/about-deloitte /articles/2014-millennial-survey-positive-impact.html.

3. Derrick Feldmann, *Inspiring The Next Generation Workforce*, Case Foundation/Achieve, November 2014, accessed August 10, 2016, http://casefoundation.org/wp-content/uploads/2014/11/ MillennialImpactReport-2014.pdf.

4. Ibid.

5. *Yum! Brands 2015 Corporate Social Responsibility Report Performance Summary*, Yum!, 2015, accessed August 18, 2016, http://www.yumcsr.com /pdf/CSR_PerformanceSummary_15.pdf.

6. Ibid.

7. *Yum! Brands 2015 Corporate Social Responsibility Report*, "Specially-Abled Restaurants," Yum!, 2015, accessed August 18, 2016, http://www.yumcsr.com /people/specially-able-restaurants.asp.

8. David Novak, "The Awesome Power of Recognition," *AMA Quarterly*, Spring 2016, 26–28.

9. *Yum! Brands 2015 Corporate Social Responsibility Report*, "Specially-Abled Restaurants."

Chapter 6

1. Art Kleiner, *The Age of Heretics: A History of the Radical Thinkers Who Reinvented Corporate Management* (San Francisco: Jossey-Bass, 2008), 3, 213.

2. "Younger Managers Rise in the Ranks: Survey Quantifies Management Shift and Reveals Challenges, Preferred Workplace Perks, and Perceived Generational Strengths and Weaknesses," Ernst & Young press release, September 3, 2013, accessed August 24, 2016, http://www.ey.com/US/en /Newsroom/News-releases/News_Younger-managers-rise-in-the-ranks.

3. Leslie Gaines-Ross and Bradley Honan, *The Social CEO: Executives Tell All*, Weber Shandwick, May 2013, accessed August 24, 2016, https://www.webershandwick.com/uploads/news/files/Social-CEO-Study.pdf.

4. Ibid.

5. Richard Branson, "Questions from Kids," Virgin, February 1, 2016, accessed August 24, 2016, https://www.virgin.com/richard-branson/questions-kids.

6. Ibid.

Acknowledgments

This book is something I've wanted to write since my first career transition from engineer to training manager. After experiencing a work environment that disabled instead of enabled me, despite being one of the best companies to work for, I embarked on a mission to modernize the workplace. *The Millennial Myth* represents a significant milestone in bringing to life the research, interviews, and experiences I've had along this path. There have been many people who have helped support me on this journey and I'd like to acknowledge a few.

Thank you to those who contributed to the case studies and stories presented: Martha Clarkson, Program Manager for Workplace Strategies at Microsoft; Alex Goryachev, Senior Director of Innovation and Strategy at Cisco; Shani Richards, Taylor Sam, and Kristina Ordanza of the University of the Pacific; Scott Young, founder of ScottHYoung.com; Ryan McCarty, Director of Community and Employee Engagement at TCC; Angela Damiani, cofounder of NEWaukee; Jonathan Barzel; Sherina Edwards; Anne Moder; Jacklyn Faith; and Rick Kramer.

I'd like to thank my mentors, who have stayed close to my work and contributed to my concepts through rich discussions. Lisa Owens, whose relationship with me started with dinner on the eve of her retirement, I cannot thank you enough for the detailed feedback, conversations, and opportunities to partner. Jennifer Kahnweiler, who I met by chance at Association for Talent Development, thanks for spending the time to mentor me and believing I was ready to write this book (and making me believe it too!). Lee Goss, whose wife saw me speak at a TEDx, thank you for helping provide invaluable boomer/gen X insight through our joint talks for Monster.com. Amy Newcomer, thanks for always working with me to improve and reinvent ideas, especially in relation to Generation

University. Lastly, Andrea Falls, who I met at TEDxPeachtree some years ago, whose creativity in thought shines in our discussions.

I'd like to thank the BK team: my editors for supporting the vision of the book, Neal Maillet and Jeevan Sivasubramanian; my production team for their detailed review, Jon Ford and Jonathan Peck; and my marketing team, Shabnam McFarland-Banerjee, Katie Sheehan, Zoe Mackey, Matt McFarland, Catherine Lengronne, and Maria Jesus Aguilo. I'd also like to thank my reviewers for their invaluable feedback: Kati Vastola, Shabnam McFarland-Banerjee, Andrea Chilcote, Jeff Kulick, and Melissa Ramos.

Last, but not least, I'd like to thank my friends and family for their continual support. Jeremy Segal, my rock and my source for calm in the deep ocean that makes up my thoughts. My mom, dad, and sister for always being there and believing in my unconventional path. Aaron Wang, for all the brainstorming, providing a workspace that was "alone but together," and letting me talk through writer's block with you. I couldn't have made this journey without the amazing people who I am fortunate enough to have in my life.

Index

About the Author

Crystal Kadakia is a lauded speaker, author, trainer, and consultant on the topics of millennials and modernizing the workplace. As the founder of Invati Consulting, her expertise is in driving the connection between millennial behavior and the design of engaging, productive modern workplaces. She is honored to be a two-time TEDx speaker as well as an Association for Talent Development "One to Watch," Chief Learning Officer "Learning in Practice," and Power 30 Under 30 awards recipient. Her consulting clients and keynote speaking audiences have included corporations, conferences, and universities such as UPS, Wells Fargo, FedEx, the Association for Talent Development (ATD), the Society for Human Resource Management (SHRM), Monster.com, General Dynamics Electric Boat, and the University of the Pacific. Crystal is also a blogger for the Huffington Post and the Human Capital Institute, as well as a Certified Coach by Coach Training Alliance. Her educational and corporate background includes a 2018 master's candidate for organizational development from Pepperdine University, a bachelor's degree in chemical engineering from the University of Texas at Austin, and a career as an engineer and training manager for a Fortune 50 company. She is currently based in Atlanta with her partner, Jeremy.

Working with Invati

Invati Consulting, founded by Crystal Kadakia, offers speaking, training, and consulting services for creating modern workplace culture based on next generation insight. If you have any questions or would like to reach out to engage Crystal's services, feel free to e-mail her at ckadakia @invaticonsulting.com with your request or go to www.invaticonsulting .com for more information.

Berrett–Koehler
Publishers

Berrett-Koehler is an independent publisher dedicated to an ambitious mission: Connecting people and ideas to create a world that works for all.

We believe that the solutions to the world's problems will come from all of us, working at all levels: in our organizations, in our society, and in our own lives. Our BK Business books help people make their organizations more humane, democratic, diverse, and effective (we don't think there's any contradiction there). Our BK Currents books offer pathways to creating a more just, equitable, and sustainable society. Our BK Life books help people create positive change in their lives and align their personal practices with their aspirations for a better world.

All of our books are designed to bring people seeking positive change together around the ideas that empower them to see and shape the world in a new way.

And we strive to practice what we preach. At the core of our approach is Stewardship, a deep sense of responsibility to administer the company for the benefit of all of our stakeholder groups including authors, customers, employees, investors, service providers, and the communities and environment around us. Everything we do is built around this and our other key values of quality, partnership, inclusion, and sustainability.

This is why we are both a B-Corporation and a California Benefit Corporation—a certification and a for-profit legal status that require us to adhere to the highest standards for corporate, social, and environmental performance.

We are grateful to our readers, authors, and other friends of the company who consider themselves to be part of the BK Community. We hope that you, too, will join us in our mission.

A BK Business Book

We hope you enjoy this BK Business book. BK Business books pioneer new leadership and management practices and socially responsible approaches to business. They are designed to provide you with groundbreaking and practical tools to transform your work and organizations while upholding the triple bottom line of people, planet, and profits. High-five!

To find out more, visit **www.bkconnection.com.**

Berrett–Koehler
Publishers

Connecting people and ideas
to create a world that works for all

Dear Reader,

Thank you for picking up this book and joining our worldwide community of Berrett-Koehler readers. We share ideas that bring positive change into people's lives, organizations, and society.

To welcome you, we'd like to offer you a free e-book. You can pick from among twelve of our bestselling books by entering the promotional code **BKP92E** here: http://www.bkconnection.com/welcome.

When you claim your free e-book, we'll also send you a copy of our e-news-letter, the *BK Communiqué*. Although you're free to unsubscribe, there are many benefits to sticking around. In every issue of our newsletter you'll find

- A free e-book
- Tips from famous authors
- Discounts on spotlight titles
- Hilarious insider publishing news
- A chance to win a prize for answering a riddle

Best of all, our readers tell us, "Your newsletter is the only one I actually read." So claim your gift today, and please stay in touch!

Sincerely,

Charlotte Ashlock
Steward of the BK Website

Questions? Comments? Contact me at bkcommunity@bkpub.com.

MIX
Paper from
responsible sources
FSC® C011935

Certified

Corporation
bcorporation.net